THINGS
NO ONE
ELSE CAN
TEACH US

ALSO BY HUMBLE THE POET

Unlearn

THINGS NO ONE ELSE CAN TEACH US

HUMBLE THE POET

HarperOne
An Imprint of HarperCollins*Publishers*

HarperOne

HarperCollins books may be purchased for educational, business, or sales promotional use. For information, please email the Special Markets Department in the US at SPsales@harpercollins.com or in Canada at HCOrder@harpercollins.com.

FIRST EDITION

Designed by Yvonne Chan

Library of Congress Cataloging-in-Publication Data

Names: Singh, Kanwer, 1981– author.
Title: Things no one else can teach us / Humble the Poet.
Description: San Francisco : Collins, 2019.
Identifiers: LCCN 2019010454| ISBN 9781443457927 (hardback) |
    ISBN 9780062905185 (hardcover) | ISBN 9780062905192 (e-book) |
    9781443457934 (e-book)
Subjects: LCSH: Self-actualization (Psychology) | Happiness. | BISAC: SELF-HELP
    / Personal Growth / Happiness. | SELF-HELP / Personal Growth / General. |
    BUSINESS & ECONOMICS / Motivational.
Classification: LCC BF637.S4 S565 2019 | DDC 155.2—dc23 LC record available
    at https://lccn.loc.gov/2019010454

Library and Archives Canada Cataloguing in Publication information is available upon request.

ISBN 978-0-06-290518-5

ISBN 978-1-4434-5792-7 (Canada)

19 20 21 22 23 LSC 10 9 8 7 6 5 4 3 2 1

CONTENTS

Introduction   1

FORTUNATELY/UNFORTUNATELY, NOTHING LASTS FOREVER

Open   13

1. Everything Is Temporary,
   so Appreciate Those You Have While You Have Them   16

2. Patience Is Making Time Your BFF   26

3. You Are Going to Die,
   and Remembering That Can Be a Good Thing   33

4. Don't Cry Because It's Over, Smile Because It Happened   39

Close   48

KNOWING YOURSELF MAKES ALL THE DIFFERENCE

Open   55

5. We Can Survive a Lot   59

6. Service to Others Is Also a Great Service to Ourselves (*Sewa*)   66

7. When We Know Our Why, Our How Gets Easier   73

8. We Gotta Pay Tuition for Life Lessons   80

Close   86

DON'T FOCUS ON THE POT OF GOLD, ENJOY THE RAINBOW

Open   93

9. Focus on the Fun, and Everything Else Will Fall into Place (and If It Doesn't, at Least You're Having Fun)   97

10. The Pot of Gold Rarely Makes the Journey Worth It   105

11. Give Yourself Permission to Dance on Different Rainbows   110

12. We All Have Different Rainbows   120

13. Often, There Is No End to the Rainbow   126

Close   132

ZOOM OUT

Open   139

14. Try to Relate to the Bad Guys in Your Story   142

15. Chapters End, but Our Story as a Whole Keeps Evolving   150

16. Judge Less, Understand More   159

17. You Aren't That Special, Embrace It   167

18. We Don't Own a Crystal Ball, so Stop Assuming the Future   172

19. Are You Being Pushed by Fear, or Pulled by Love?   178

Close   184

ZOOM IN

Open   191

20. Life Isn't Black and White, There's Plenty of Gray in Between   193

21. Don't Be So Hyperbolic (That's a Big Word for Dramatic)   201

22. Detach Your Self-Worth from Your Choices   206

Close   212

LIMIT YOUR SELF-PITY

Open   219

23. Caution: Social Media Is a Playground for Self-Pity   221

24. Self-Pity Is Easy and Convenient like Fast Food
    (and Just as Unhealthy)   228

25. We Don't Scream "Why Me?!" During the Good Times,
    so Don't Scream It During the Bad   234

26. Turn Rejection into Invitation   238

27. Self-Pity Feeds Our Insecurities
    (and That Leaves Us Bitter and Angry)   245

28. Getting Offended Is a Form of Self-Pity   254

Close   260

THERE'S NO WIN OR LOSE, THERE'S ONLY WIN OR LEARN

Open   267

29. Stop Calling Them Failures, Start Calling Them Teachers   269

30. Not Everyone We Lose Is a Loss   276

31. We Can Lose More Trying to Win   281

32. Freedom Is Having Nothing to Lose   288

33. There Are No Time Machines, so Fix It Next Time   294

Close   298

Outro   303

Acknowledgments   307

INTRODUCTION

In 1998 Snoop Dogg released his third album, *Da Game Is to Be Sold, Not to Be Told*, and I remember seeing the ridiculously blinged-out album cover and thinking to myself, "What does that mean? Why can't you just tell me *Da Game*? Why do I have to buy it?"

I've always loved hip hop, and as a youngster, I soaked in as much of it as I could, reading the lyrics and jumping on internet forums to share my thoughts and immerse myself in those of other aficionados. Those early years made me realize how amazing writers and hip hop artists were. I knew then if I wanted to explore my talents as a writer, it needed to be through rap.

So I spent the first years of adulthood writing my own hip hop songs, giving myself the name Poet to make me sound smarter, classier, and more acceptable. As the journey of sharing my work with the world began, my written words began to connect much more than any song I recorded. That's when I began to flirt with the idea of becoming a writer, well, a REAL writer.

I dreamed of the day I'd become a full-fledged real writer. You know, the type of writer who was published with a major publisher. The type of writer who spent most of his time traveling the world, having promiscuous sex, finding inspiration in cloud formations, and somehow interpreting all those experiences into words* that would be celebrated beyond my life.

How romantic it would be to live the life of a real writer. Early morning writing sessions with a typewriter by a lake and perfectly developed ideas floating from my head onto the page. I would see a leaf fall from a tree and convert that moment into an epic chapter about change, expectations, and the circle of life.

I told myself that if I ever got the opportunity to become a real writer, I would take the money the publishers gave me and find a quiet apartment in a quiet city in a quiet corner of the planet and write my epic first, and last, novel. Then I'd go into hiding like J. D. Salinger, live off the royalties, and once in a while reply to letters from high school students who were forced to study my book for their English independent study projects.

Instead, when I signed my contract with HarperCollins, I wrote the bulk of this book on my mother's dining table at home in Toronto. I walked around the same neighborhood I grew up in, taking familiar routes where the nostalgia fades and gentrification continues to thrive. I politely avoided my wonderful editors' recommendations to write an outline** and spent an entire summer free writing. I then spent the rest of the fall and winter rewriting from scratch, after failing to find a thread that joined all my summer jumbles together.***

Being a full-time creative came with other unglamorous challenges. Poor posture and neglecting to do the most basic stretches flared up a preexisting lower back injury, so sitting for more than an hour, whether at my dining room table, in a movie theater, or on a

---

* And Instagram captions.
** Real writers don't need outlines, I thought.
*** Lesson One: Write an outline.

private jet, resulted in pain for the rest of the day. Irony never loses its sense of humor. Sitting down to write became more taxing on my body than my previous life as an elementary school teacher, when I stood all day in front of a class.

I experienced profound creative moments during the writing process late at night, only to forget them in the morning. I began to keep a notebook to flesh out ideas when they struck, but I couldn't understand my own chicken scratch when it was time to revisit.

Yeah, the glorious life of "real writer" continues to elude me, or maybe I just overly romanticized it in my head. When those romantic ideas didn't match the life I had in front of me, I began feeling disappointed, betrayed, and generally crappy. In order to feel better, I had to let go of the expectations I had and open myself up to finding, discovering, and creating beauty in the circumstances in front of me and not the fantasies between my ears. And that's what this book is about.

That's probably what the story of all of our lives is about.

We all know that great moments fade quickly and bad moments seem to last forever. We promise ourselves that hitting that next milestone will make us feel better, but after a few days, we're off chasing the next high.

We're always waiting for that day when everything we've struggled with, everything we've suffered for, everything that's ever left us feeling empty is finally magically fixed and we can live happily ever after. We forget that this sparkly moment in our fantasies always has a day after, which presents us with new challenges and problems all over again. It's a cycle we don't want to acknowledge, and one that leaves us feeling either lost and hopeless or numb and unmotivated.

We look to others to help "fix" these problems and feelings— maybe a wellness guru who combines common sense with encouraging words on how we can use our personal power to make it all better. The guru's words feel good as we're reading them, but they don't last long enough to keep us away from the bookstore, where we chase a new fix of hollow hope.

There's a reason we keep finding ourselves in these patterns. When we continue to expect our problems, our mindsets, and our situations to get solved by something, or someone, other than ourselves, we are always going to be disappointed. The truth is, we are responsible for ourselves, and that includes the way we see things. This sounds like tough love, and maybe it is, but it's also hopeful.

You are the only person capable of creating real change in your life. And you can feel that real change only when you can feel it within you.

I'm not a real writer because I have a book published by a major publisher, or even because you're reading my stuff, or even because I'm good at it. I'm a real writer because I shifted my perspective about that definition. It's not about the quiet writing corner or the fancy publishing contract or the stereotypical promiscuous lifestyle of a tortured genius. It's about the fact that I sat down and, despite my insecurities, lethargy, and short attention span, I *wrote*. That's what real writers do: they write.* But I realized this only once I recognized my ability to see things differently. And here's the important part: I had to figure that out myself. No one else could do it for me, and no amount of advice or number of wellness gurus and motivational quotes could have taught me.

I had to explore, experience, and face the things no one else could teach me.

---

* Especially when you think about all those people you know who always talk about getting around to writing a book, but never do.

The beauty of changing the way we see things is that we find ourselves in a position to discover and create the beauty we seek, no matter what's happening in our lives, no matter how dark those moments feel.

> *In the depth of winter, I finally learned that within me there lay an invincible summer.*
>
> —Albert Camus, "Return to Tipasa"

So let's talk about those dark moments—the heartbreaks, the losses, the embarrassments, the contradictions, and the moments when everything blew up in our faces. Let's treat them like that leaf falling from a tree and see whether we can find moments of magic, silver linings, lessons, and beauty in them.

Let's talk about the things no one else can teach us, particularly the big one that it's possible to start seeing things differently. Like Camus, we can all find the invincible summer within even the coldest of winter nights.

These are my stories, my darkest moments, my happiest of accidents, and my journey to see beyond what was right in front of me. I, like you, have made some bone-headed mistakes, and then repeated them a half dozen times before noticing a pattern and trying to learn from those mistakes. The purpose of these stories isn't to show you how to live or to tell you what to do like the wellness gurus I just scoffed at. It's to help you realize you're not alone in the challenges you face and to help you remember that you can transform those challenges with a new perspective. It's possible to see the treasure that was always hiding among the trash.

We see ourselves in the stories of others and can free ourselves by writing the story of our own lives. I share my stories not only to help you figure out yours, but to also continue to make sense and find beauty in mine. A voice in my head continues to tell me that my stories aren't worth sharing and that it's egotistical to assume anyone would care to read them. But another voice is emerging, a voice that reminds me that we're all in this together and that sharing my challenges and experiences, and the lessons I have learned from them, will contribute to a world beyond myself. After all, storytelling has been an essential tool for our evolution as a species.

Maybe being a great writer doesn't include money, sex, fame, and travel. Maybe, just like a construction worker or a Starbucks barista, my skills are best used in service to others.

The more deeply we dive into our own stories, the more we feel like we're going through it alone. **But I'm here to remind you that you're not alone, even though we each have to do the work ourselves.** The deeper we dive, the more beauty we can discover as well. No one else shares our unique experiences, and therefore no one else can show us the light at the end of the tunnels we dig; we can only share our stories and remind ourselves that we already have everything we need to find that light.

These are the things no one else can teach us.

We all have the unlimited power to shift our perspective, and with that, the unlimited power to change the way we feel about life. This isn't a manual for fixing your life; I couldn't write one for you even if I wanted to. I can only share how I learned from the experiences I had, and how they taught me to better my life. Through my sharing, I hope you think back on your moments of good, bad, and boring to find, discover, and create something of value from them. Many of those experiences weren't pleasant, and you may not want to revisit them, but the discomfort, pain, and overall shitty feeling that came from those experiences is the price we all have to pay to gain that wisdom. In some circles, that wisdom is referred to as *game.*

Da Game Is to Be Sold, Not to Be Told

All the experiences we go through in life are our lessons, all the people we meet are our teachers. What we learn is what we earn from those experiences, and this book is here simply to help you see, discover, and create the silver lining that's always been there so you don't discard the unpleasant moments as things you want to forget. Everything we go through is important and puts us up on game to better ourselves and the way we feel moving forward. **Wisdom can't be told or taught by anyone else; only we can mine the jewels of wisdom ourselves.** That's what Snoop was getting at, and that's what Albert Camus celebrated before him.

That invincible summer doesn't require us to have certain experiences; it requires us only to open ourselves up to life in a certain way, to see things beyond what's on the surface.

I can't promise you "happily ever after," and that's not something you should expect or promise yourself either. I can, however, share my stories of figuring shit out on my own by changing the way I perceived things. I encourage you to use a new lens—one not of blind optimism but of empowered opportunism in which you recognize that you have the ability to turn any situation that appears to be shitty into something much sweeter. Once you've embraced that power, you won't be as afraid to face new challenges and setbacks that life will undoubtedly present to you. Simply having a better attitude toward them will show you the sugar among any shit.

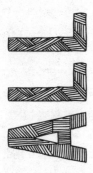

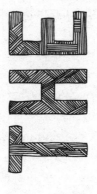

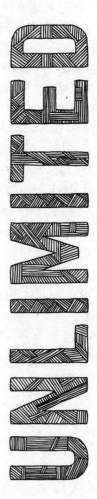

WE ALL HAVE THE UNLIMITED

POWER TO SHIFT OUR PERSPECTIVE.

FORTUNATELY/
UNFORTUNATELY,
NOTHING LASTS
FOREVER

Enter

Summers seem shorter
Winters get longer
Friendships end with the seasons
And we won't always welcome spring
Time stops standing still for us, and the happy-ever-afters never
   happen
It's terrifying
Everyone I know and love will be dead
It's comforting
Everyone I resent and hate will be dead
All ashes
How can we have something everlasting
In a world where nothing ever lasts
Everything comes to pass
Everything is temporary
Even us
How fortunate and unfortunate for us
Death is the only promise

OPEN

It's frustrating to know that the new outfit you just bought, the one that brings you so much excitement and confidence, is one day going to sit unloved at the back of your closet. When you get around to spring cleaning, you'll look at it, embarrassed, and wonder, "Why did I buy that? What was I thinking?" Shit gets old very quickly; nothing stands the test of time anymore. Companies make stuff to break so we'll buy the next generation of stuff, which will also break. This makes the world, and life, feel that much more temporary.

Mother Nature also created us with a form of built-in obsolescence: death. We have an expiration date, and that also makes the world, and life, feel that much more temporary. The longer we live, the more we experience death, in and around us. Many of my childhood heroes are dead, like my grandmother, Nani. I'll never get to feel her leathery, wrinkly hands again. Growing up, absorbed in her cuddles, I thought she would be here forever. But she wasn't, and as I stood in the hospital room staring at her lifeless body, I thought of my mother and father and how, if everything plays out as it should, I'll be watching them pass away too one day.

Nothing lasts forever.

The fact that life is temporary—the happiness, the joy, the hope, the fear, the pain, the sorrow, the victories, the defeats—is the most comforting and terrifying fact of existence.

It always feels like the bad shit pauses at its worst moments, while all the good stuff crumbles into the everyday.

"Nothing lasts forever" sucks when we think of the good stuff, but it's oddly comforting when we think of the bad. You've fought the urge to get up to pee during a movie, knowing the credits will eventually roll and you'll be free to leave your seat without missing anything. You've sat through boring lectures, silly arguments, and never-ending weddings, knowing that these, too, will at some point wrap up. The temporary things in life have brought you peace before. Your heartbreaks have been temporary, your injuries have been temporary, your confusions, resentments, anger, and fears have all been temporary.

Still, realizing that nothing we know and cherish today will last forever can be difficult. We're on borrowed time. My mother says our number of breaths has been predetermined.* Irrespective of the allegory, analogy, or belief, we're not going to last. Not in the short term or the grand scheme.

That realization might make us want to hide in the nearest corner, assume the fetal position, and scream, "Why bother doing anything? What's the point if it's all going to end?"

So now that I've massaged your existential dread, I'm supposed to teach you to find beauty in this world of temporary, right? Wrong. You've had your near-death experiences and promised to live a new life, only to fall back into your whack habits a few days later. You've lost things that mattered to you, people who mattered to you, and you're still here, knowing that one day you'll also be lost; no one makes it out alive.

What I *can* do is help you see how recognizing that everything is temporary can take a lot of the pressure off and help you jump

---

* And possibly written on our foreheads with some sort of metaphysical invisible ink.

headfirst into life, finding more reasons to be grateful, to connect with others, and most important, to connect with yourself. In the past I've written about letting go to gain more. This time, let's talk about how much we lose from holding on. Let's talk about the gifts we receive when we lose, and how all of this can help us clean out our closets and keep only what's most important. Let's talk about how we should value something *because* it's temporary, including our own lives.

Looking at life through the lens of time shows us how patience is a superpower. Loss feeds love and encourages us to look at the bigger picture.

Nothing lasts forever, and that's both tragic and comic, depending on how we look at it—so how we look at it, our perspective, is the thing we can, and should, control. We can give ourselves a facepalm when we look at that old outfit, or we can try it on and dance around the room summoning up the spirits and smiles of yesterday—a beautiful reminder of how far we've come.

1

EVERYTHING IS TEMPORARY, SO APPRECIATE THOSE YOU HAVE WHILE YOU HAVE THEM

Shit had hit the fan. My rap career had launched, but not at the rate I'd expected. I had moved into a condo I couldn't afford the prior year, planning to pay for it with future funds I assumed would come pouring in. Suddenly I realized I'd spent twelve months sitting in smoke-filled studios, making music whenever inspiration (or the weed) hit me, having no idea how to pay my mortgage. I was broke and uninspired.

Things needed to be different. Not only did I have to audit my bank account, but I had to audit the people I spent my time with. We all go through these times in life, when we have to slow things down, re-evaluate, and do some spring cleaning. Yet for me, this spring cleaning was less about holistic renewal and more about clearing my professional path. I decided that if someone wasn't helping me get to where I needed to be, then that person most likely was getting in my way. I didn't make any proclamations or write anybody a Dear John letter, thus liberating myself from their harmful clutches. I didn't say a thing to anybody; I just stopped engaging with people who I felt were standing in my way rather than helping me and I began to focus more on myself.

I started with the people in my life who were less than inspiring, even toxic. The ones making decisions that didn't feel responsible or sustainable to me. You know the people I'm talking about: the ones who feel like more of a chore or an obligation than a friend.

Purging these kinds of people from my life had immediate benefits. It freed up my time and energy so I was able to spend time with people and things that actually excited me, rather than drained me. Slowly, I cleansed my personal life of all the whack people I was spending time with. It was instantly liberating for me, but shedding friends also became addictive.

I didn't stop there.

After getting rid of all my bad friends, I started looking at my good friends. The ones who were pleasant sources of energy yet sought out comfort through conformity and avoiding risk at every turn. They were well meaning but expressed their worry whenever I shared my nontraditional thoughts and ideas about taking risks and coloring outside the lines. I was on an entrepreneurial journey, and as sweet as those people were, I realized that I no longer had things in common with many of them. I decided I needed to surround myself with people I wanted to be like: self-employed, empowered, risk-embracing. In other words, I wanted to be around people only if they could help and inspire me on my journey.

No friend's feelings were harmed in the making of Humble the Poet, at least not in my self-indulgent, apathetic eyes. Because of my financial strain and the slowdown in my inspiration, I felt like I was in "sink-or-swim" mode, and even the good people in my life were slowing me down.

If you want to go fast, go alone . . .

—African proverb

I wanted to go fast. I wanted out of the hole I was in. I wanted fresh air. I was sick of being broke, sick of losing, sick of being betrayed by people after believing their empty promises. I needed to figure things out by myself.

Fuck everybody else.

Everybody else, unfortunately, included Boomerang.

Boomerang was a friend of a friend. Though that friend disappeared abruptly after being caught making uninspiring decisions, Boomerang remained.

Boomerang and I soon got to know each other on a deeper level. He was a sweet guy, and we had a lot in common. He was making beats as a side hustle and loved a lot of the same music I did, and in the later stages of our friendship, we bonded over the betrayal we both felt from our former friend.

But Boomerang worked in insurance, or finance—something to do with money and sales. I didn't take the time to understand because none of it sounded like it was beneficial to me, the aspiring rapper and artist.

We wouldn't hang out one-on-one often, yet Boomerang came to every event I threw, alongside our ragtag band of creatives. He was always there, front and center, alongside other artists who were integral to the creative moment we were all a part of. He put in the time and the effort.

Every so often he would send me a message asking me to hang out with him, and I would be either out of town or too busy working on something to be social. I always told him I would get back to him soon, but never did.

Boomerang never took it personally. He still showed up at the events, still showed love, and still regularly reached out to check in.

One cold January night, right before I was headed to LA for a few weeks for work, I contacted him at the last minute to hang out. I was in his neighborhood and figured it was convenient to stop by. We spent less than an hour shooting the shit and catching up. I didn't stay long because I had to prepare for my trip, and I was basically squeezing him in before heading to the next thing. But we had a good time: he loved hearing stories and always asked the kinds of questions that made me know he was genuinely interested. I realized that Boomerang's only intention was to hang out with good people. Just as he reached out to me regularly to catch up, he made efforts to stay in contact with all his friends. He, like everybody else, just wanted to be around great energy.

Even though I enjoyed the short time I spent with him that January night, at that point in my life I felt I couldn't afford to be around people who weren't directly serving my ambitions.

I would get daily requests from people to sit down for a coffee to discuss a new project or idea or to pitch me a business venture. Some people just wanted to show their social media followers that they knew me. I viewed these requests in one of two ways: either I didn't feel those people were helping me to get where I wanted to go, or I worried they were trying to use me. I got bit in the ass a few too many times, so I developed a generous layer of paranoia when trying to figure out people's intentions. These two reactions to people approaching me—for business and for friendship—led me to avoid most people, and I focused my energy on spending time with creatives and people in my industry, who I felt were going to help me get my own stuff off the ground. Boomerang had some creative ideas, but he never pursued them on a serious level. So even though the time I spent with him made me happy, I didn't prioritize him. I didn't see the point.

The irony was, in my relentless pursuit of the right kind of people to surround myself with, I ended up becoming the kind of person I was trying to avoid.

In July of that year, I put out the music video for my song "H.A.I.R," and Boomerang was one of the first to message and congratulate me on the release. He sent nothing but love and asked whether we could link up soon. I told him I was out of town until late August. I never followed up with him when I returned.

"Congrats on the new Video man, it's Fire!"

"Thank You man"

"Are you back in the city? we need to hang out and catch up"

"I'll be back in a few weeks, near the end of August, I'll hit you up when I am"

"Okay cool, we'll do the weekend, weekdays are busy for me"

"Awesome"

Those few texts would be the last time we connected.

In September, Boomerang suddenly collapsed at home and was admitted to the ICU. After a short stint in a coma, he passed away.

He was gone.

There was no second chance. Boomerang always got the short end of the stick from me. I couldn't appreciate that somebody might be thinking about me and might actually want to spend time with me, regardless of any networking or professional currency I had. I could make a list of all the famous people I went out of my way to be around, hoping to extract some wisdom, opportunity, or introduction to something or someone that would further me on my journey, but very few of them felt awesome to be around. Boomerang felt awesome to be around, but for some reason that wasn't enough for me.

I was a terrible friend to someone who was nothing but wonderful to me, and I don't want that to happen again, not to me, or to anyone reading this book. I still have those last texts from my phone, and when I look at them, I know I could have contacted him when I got back at the end of August, but I didn't, and now he's not here anymore.

We forget/ignore/avoid mortality for so many reasons, and when those close to us pass away, we wake up, but only temporarily, before we reset to our unappreciative defaults.

I don't want to blame Los Angeles for all of this since I'm the one who didn't make my friend a priority, but I do know that the LA environment contributed to my decisions at that time. The "what can you do for me" mindset is dripping out of the palm trees. In Hollywood, I saw the rewards of success, and like everyone else, I wanted a piece of it. I smothered this greed in good intentions and elaborate justifications, but the truth is, I really just hoped achieving success would make me feel better about myself.

It didn't. It wouldn't. How could it?

I didn't realize how much being in Los Angeles affected my priorities until I left and took an active break from that environment.

The uncomfortable reality is that any connection with a friend could possibly be the last. But that uncomfortable reality is also a good lens for viewing the world: if we kept this in mind, we would treat the people in our lives with more care. Remembering that the people in our lives won't be here forever is the best way to motivate us to be as wonderful to them as possible, while they're still here. It's tricky, since we're not really wired to remember this fact, but when we make the active effort to keep it in mind, beautiful choices come from that effort.

But we don't.

When we chase ambition, we focus on what we don't have and spend less time appreciating the things and people we do have. As a result, we further isolate ourselves from each other, assuming that everything we experience and everyone we know will always be here. **The people we have won't always be here, so let's not deprive ourselves of their presence simply because we're too caught up in wanting more of some other stuff.** That other stuff won't last either—nothing does. So let's appreciate who and what we have while we still have it. If we're not happy with what we have, we won't be very happy with all that we get.

I made time to beat myself up after Boomerang's death. I was unforgiving, frustrated, and unkind. I said a lot of mean things to myself, but more important than needing to hear it, I needed to say it. At that point it was the closest thing to tears I would let flow out of me.

Once I got it out, I started making a list of other people in my life who, like Boomerang, may not have been well versed on my hustle but were wonderful for my spirit. I took that list and put reminders in my phone to reach out to those people every fifty days. Inspired by Boomerang, I started with a simple, "Hey, how you been?" I would listen to the answer, ask more questions, and then speak some more.

As time went on, life consumed me again, but those reminders still buzzed, dinged, and beeped, encouraging me to reach out to friends I've made around the world. The more I do this, the better life feels. I put our hangouts into my calendar because if something's not in my schedule, it's not a priority. I no longer said, "Sorry, I'm headed to LA." Instead I said, "Hey, I'll be heading to LA in eight days, let's squeeze something in."

This has slowed down my output just a bit, but what am I working for if I have no one in my life worth sharing it with? Focusing on less has also allowed me to dive deeper into things that excite me instead of simply trying to keep my lips above water with an overwhelming TO-DO list.

"What can you do for me?" always leads to isolation. And that isolation can't be helped with a juicy bank account. If anything, success will only amplify the loneliness. We all want connection, and we think being desirable will finally scratch that itch, so we chase things like success and accolades to make ourselves more desirable to others. The problem with that is, if we don't improve how we feel about ourselves, it won't matter how many others desire us. We'll start thinking less of them for wanting to be around someone like us.

After Boomerang died, I realized I didn't want to play that game anymore. What for? What other people can do for me will rarely get me out of bed, because there's no meaning and purpose behind it other than stroking my feeble ego. I realized that I felt connected, significant, and seen by others when I took the time to ask, "What can I do for you?"

Although my time with Boomerang was temporary, his impact won't be. Boomerang's life gave me a model for how to make time for people I care about, and his death gave me a sharp reminder of how much prioritizing friendship matters. His approach to friendship wasn't a deep secret or anything revolutionary, but it took his passing for me to take the steps to implement it in my own life.

Boomerang's death challenged me to find real, sustainable solutions to problems I only talked about in the past. Words mean nothing if actions don't follow. Instead of selfishly chasing my ambitions, now I make time for the people I care about.

> . . . if you want to go far, go together.
> —The rest of that African proverb

If I could say one more thing to my friend Boomerang, it would be: *I miss you man. I'm sorry I wasn't a better friend and didn't make more time for you. I'm going to learn from my past and make a better future for anyone who crosses my path. I think about you every day, and thoughts of you make this life feel a little less lonely. I will honor your beautiful memory through action and service and hold myself to a standard higher than my old self-indulgent ways.*

Thank you for setting that bar.

REMEMBERING THAT
THE PEOPLE IN OUR LIVES
WON'T BE HERE FOREVER IS
THE BEST WAY TO MOTIVATE
US TO BE AS WONDERFUL
TO THEM AS POSSIBLE,
WHILE THEY'RE STILL HERE.

2

PATIENCE IS MAKING TIME YOUR BFF

I had started visiting New York regularly for work, and it was love at first sight. The energy, the people, the endless sources of stimulation and distraction—everything about the city was exciting. I felt like I was becoming a cooler person just by being there. But then I was violently robbed on a small street between Brooklyn and Queens in the middle of the night, and that love affair ended abruptly.

The trauma from that experience stayed with me. Once the cuts and bruises healed from the attack, I still found myself tensing up and freezing whenever people got physically close to me.

I hated that this experience changed me: I felt like I had lost a part of myself. I was constantly anxious and often involuntarily relived the experience. So many things were triggering. It felt exhausting.

So when I was approached by a stranger in the New York subway at midnight several years later, I had the choice to either freeze and not engage or to do something different.

I had just finished my first sold-out performance in Manhattan and was taking the subway home after dinner with a cousin. Subway stops in New York are full of character, and full of characters. Most people drown each other out with the music in their ears, and I did the same. I was waiting for a train at a station that was particularly old and run-down. I thought of the Ninja Turtles as I saw rats scurry across the tracks.

As I stared at the rats, singing the "Turtle Power" theme song in my head, an older gentleman approached me, wearing clothes out of 1990s Harlem. Instead of walking by, he stopped and said something to me. I didn't hear him with my headphones on, and as I took them off and was about to ask him to repeat what he'd said—since I thought he might be asking directions—he continued speaking.

"I see angels and demons around you."

The postattack anxious voice inside me said, *Umm, okay . . . I'm uncomfortable.*

"I see them all around you, you're an angel," he said, before turning away.

It was close to midnight at a subway station in Harlem, so what else could I expect? I didn't think much of it, but I still had my guard up, because, as I had already learned, anything can happen.

The train arrived and I got in and took a seat. The older gentleman walked around the empty car and then sat down across from me. He stared at me, eyes wide, mouth half open, like a child absorbed in a favorite TV show. He looked at me intensely, but I didn't feel any uncomfortable energy. Although I felt confused, I gave the man a smile, which prompted him to speak again.

"They're all around the car, angels and demons, I can see them, you don't see them?!"

I spoke out loud for the first time. "I don't," I replied honestly.

"You need to know you're an angel, you have to watch out for those fucking demons."

I have a few exes who would disagree with that assessment, but thank you?

Some passengers tried to ignore what was happening, while others peeked over their phones, finding our exchange interesting. I was still fifteen stops away from my destination, but something inside me trusted this stranger enough to ask him a question, to start a conversation. There was something genuine in him, and something in me that made me less afraid than I'd felt in months.

"How do you know I'm an angel?" I asked, feeling less fearful. The anxiety was still there, but what had also been growing was frustration from being so closed off to everyone. It was isolating and suffocating. I never wore my trust issues as an identifying marker. I never wanted to have any trust issues to begin with, but it was hard to be open to others, even when I tried. This night, however, and this gentleman for some reason, was making it just a little bit easier.

"See the light around you? It's a different color, a different color from the rest of these fucking demons. Can I sit beside you?"

"Sure."

My internal anxious voice returned, *Why did you say that?*

He sat down in the seat next to mine, his eyes sincere and purposeful.

"There are so many evil beings pretending to be angels, but they can't change the color of their light. They pretend to preach the truth, but they're liars, robbing people blind. You have to protect yourself from these people."

"I will, man," I replied. I felt I needed to reassure him, but I also still strongly felt the need to protect myself.

"Can I hold your hand?" he asked unexpectedly.

"Sure," I agreed, surprising even myself.

The anxiety was coming back. *C'mon Kanwer, use your brain, he's going to ask you for money any second now.*

As he held my hand he closed his eyes and said, "I need you to

28

be safe from these demons. They're afraid of your light and will come after you. I pray for your protection."

How many strangers are praying for my protection? He seemed sincere, and I felt safer and warmer than I expected. He gave me the feeling I had when I was four years old, sleeping nose to nose with my grandmother, kissing her wrinkled cheeks and cuddling her until I fell asleep. When she spoke to me without her dentures, it was as unclear as this man's Harlem accent. Yet his energy felt familiar, it felt nice. I don't want to say I felt his love, but I did feel his calm.

Other passengers were invested in our story as well. No one else seemed concerned, only intrigued.

As the train slowed at the next stop, he kissed my hand, told me to stay safe, and to keep my eyes open. Then he disappeared through the closing subway doors and out of my life. I was overwhelmed at that moment; I put my headphones back on and instinctively took a deep breath. Surprisingly, I still felt calm—no anxiety, no awkwardness, just peace. The two remaining riders on the train gave me a look that I took as a giant "Whoa!" as they exited the car at the next stop.

The moment was over. The man hadn't asked me for anything, other than to stay safe. I had spent that whole trip to New York on Defcon 5, keys clenched between my knuckles, back against the wall, overly paranoid, and that all melted away, with one kiss on my hand.

Maybe it was a fragment of my grandmother's energy, or maybe that man could see angels and demons, or maybe it was all bullshit. But it wasn't bullshit to me.

My experience with that man made me feel calm, and my anxiety hasn't returned since. As someone who doesn't dabble too much in the supernatural, I do respect energy and vibes, and that man, with his nineties throwback outfit and heavy Harlem slang, had some of the purest, most authentic energy I've ever experienced from a stranger.

I believe his purpose wasn't to make me feel calm, but rather to show me that I had healed from the past trauma of the robbery and could now push my limits a little bit more and open myself up to others once again. I'd chosen to ask him a question, which was a step—putting myself out there—that I'd held off on taking for months.

I didn't walk away from that experience thinking I had to protect myself as some prophetic being. Instead, I walked away pleasantly surprised, and proud that I'd regained a sense of my old self, the guy who wanted to continue exploring the universe through everyone he met. Getting beat up and robbed had temporarily suspended those adventures, but after a few years, I was ready to open myself back up to the world.

My real guardian angel in this story was time. **We never fully get over traumas, and as much as we heal, scars will remain. That doesn't mean we need to view those scars as reminders of our injuries; instead, we can see them as proof of our resilience.**

We don't have to trust others when they come into our worlds; we just have to trust ourselves to handle whatever happens. I've been cheated by people I loved, scammed by those I considered family, and beaten up and robbed by kids. But I don't want to lose the opportunity for magic moments of connection to occur, and that means I must be open and welcoming to them. Beautiful winds won't take us anywhere if we don't have our sails open.

Time was the friend that helped me heal, slowly but surely, and time showed me I could get back to who I was and that I didn't need to define myself through my past traumas. All I needed to do was be patient and know that my choices in the meantime could make things better or worse.

I could have told that gentleman to fuck off, gotten up and changed seats, or even passively kept my earbuds in, pretending not to hear him. Looking back, I'm glad I didn't. Sometimes when we're injured, we have to lean in to the pain a bit to get stronger.

BEAUTIFUL WINDS
WON'T TAKE US ANYWHERE
IF WE DON'T HAVE
OUR SAILS OPEN.

3

YOU ARE GOING TO DIE, AND REMEMBERING THAT CAN BE A GOOD THING

I believe that even when we are in moments of misery and self-pity, the universe will offer us totems—lessons that pull us out of our selfish orbits and help us see the bigger picture. The most recent totem gifted to me was a puddle. The puddle found me as I worked on a very ambitious six-month music video for a track I recorded titled *I Will*.

The video features multiple tableaus, each telling a different story. It was inspired by the visual images of gangs in the 1979 film *The Warriors*, but I threw a little twist on it, with one gang being represented by the toughest group of people I know: cancer thrivers. I use the word *thrivers* instead of *survivors* because the women I worked with are doing much more than just surviving. They are fighting a daily battle against a horrific disease, but also confronting the reality that many of us work so hard to avoid: the fact that time is running out. We put out a call and found four strong women who were willing to show their battle scars on camera. While we were setting up, I spoke with them all, and my curiosity trumped my discretion and tact.

"How does life feel different now?" I asked, unsure whether I was being too forward or insensitive.

"Well, cancer taught me how to fall in love with puddles," replied a woman named Anne Marie. "I never noticed puddles before my diagnosis. I was too busy worrying about all the other useless shit life throws at us. The moment I found out it all might go away, I started noticing beauty in the simplest things, like the reflections in a puddle."

Anne Marie's cancer took a lot from her, but she had an amazing partner who was by her side during recovery and at the shoot; their love inspired me beyond words. It was almost as if the cancer had done some reorganizing with her life, leaving only what really mattered, with room to notice all the beauty that was hidden before.

The type of beauty found only in puddles.

We all experience loss and tragic news. Many of us are fortunate that those situations aren't as intense as cancer, but it's not about comparing our suffering; it's about the perspectives we have when that suffering hits us. When everything is going well and according to plan, we often sleepwalk through life, focused on our repetitious days of routine and boredom. When something unexpected strikes, we're suddenly jolted out of our comfort zone, often ill prepared, unsure of what just happened, heart racing a mile a minute.

Facing death is a great alarm clock. Being aware of our mortality, even when things are going well, is a great way to avoid pressing the snooze button.

I had spent that day running around like a chicken without a head, and Anne Marie's words stopped me in my tracks. We stress about things because we think they're important, but are they really that important when it's all said and done? I had so much going on that it was impossible for me to see any light at the end of the tunnel; I was caving myself in. I started taking an inventory of all the things I was spending my time, energy, and focus on, and I asked myself, "Would this be worth it if today were the last day of my life?" Then I went even deeper and asked, "Is this a better use of my time than enjoying a sun-kissed sky or beautiful puddle?"

I stacked my life up with useless shit only because I forgot I wouldn't be here forever. The important stuff was supposed to happen "after"—but after what? There is no better time to enjoy life than the present, because that present is all we have. We create imaginary timelines and assume we'll still be here to see everything play out. Anne Marie's words inspired me to reevaluate my timelines and priorities. I acknowledged that if something wasn't bringing me joy, then it needed to take a back seat in my life.

People with serious health conditions, like cancer, have to shorten their timelines for the things they want in life. Goals can no longer be left to "someday," because that day may never come. But this rule applies to us all; even eighty years is a short period of time in the grand scheme of things.

For people like Anne Marie, cancer lights a fire under them to value their time and spend whatever amount they have left on their own terms. It gifts them a perspective we all could benefit from: to focus only on the things that really matter to us and to abandon playing it safe. The sky is always painted beautifully before the sun sets, but we rarely make time to enjoy it, unless we plan an elaborate vacation to a sandy destination, pretending that the sun is somehow different there, more deserving of our attention.

Things aren't black or white, good or bad, positive or negative—a lot of space exists in between, and when it comes to birth and death, our existence is that in-between space. While we're alive the possibilities are enormous, but culture, society, and tradition have us thinking that life has to be lived a certain way. Will any of that matter if we remember our days are numbered? **Sometimes it takes great loss to remind us of what we have.** That loss also makes room for us to see more things that matter, like puddles. Anne Marie helped me see this, because although she prioritized the beauty of puddles, she still participates in life's regularly scheduled programming—but she's now doing it wearing a new set of glasses, finding beauty in all the small things while still getting the biggest things done. She doesn't allow self-pity to prevent her from being in the game.

I don't know what it feels like to have such a deadly disease. I've never had to take cocktails of medications just to get out of bed, and I haven't lost my beard* to chemotherapy. Those experiences sound very difficult, and I wouldn't dare disrespect these thrivers by even trying to imagine how it feels.

But you don't have to get cancer to be a thriver; you can thrive right now. None of us is going to make it out alive, and remembering that helps to put things into perspective.

Cancer forced Anne Marie to remember she was going to die and inspired her to notice something as simple as the beautiful reflections in a puddle, which in turn reminds her that she's still alive. If we all remember our mortality, we'll find more in life to celebrate, and the things that cause us the most stress may lose a bit of strength.

A friend once said to me, "Our problems are only real because we forget we're going to die." I'm not going to ask you to be dramatic and assume that today is the last day of your life, so you can figure out what's really important. We don't need to stare death in the eyes

---

* The source of my power.

to realize that. We just have to sit down for twenty minutes with a pen and pad and make a list of what's important to us.

Sometimes when things feel too heavy, I ask myself, "Will this matter in three hundred years?" and I think about the fact that no one I know will be around then—none of their judgments, opinions, debts, or grudges—and that I should enjoy this journey while I'm still healthy enough to do so. In three hundred years it won't matter that I wasn't invited to this or that event or included on this or that list or was able to connect with this or that person. It won't matter that I showed up wearing a mustard stain on my outfit or that I didn't proofread my text message before I hit "send." Figuring out what will matter in three hundred years results in a much shorter list—almost next to nothing.

It's great to have ambitions for the future, but let's add some short-term and immediate things to look forward to as well so we're not deferring our entire life to "someday." **Let's enjoy the puddles, our loved ones, and all the roses we'd like to smell.** Anne Marie didn't quit her day job and become a nihilist; she embraced life even more and dedicated more time to helping others do the same. She didn't find a silver lining in her diagnosis; she discovered a puddle— and created one from it: after she was in remission, she founded TheseAreMyScars.com to share her cancer experiences to inspire and educate others.

I'm not going to pretend that staring at a puddle on the street engulfed forever me in a Zen state. I still stress over petty and impermanent things. But I have received renewed inspiration to take more control when those stresses become too much, and instead of drowning myself in a bottle, or pills, or another person, I dive into a puddle, and things feel a little better. A little better is a step up from a little worse, and those baby steps can add up, so splash your feet.

THINGS AREN'T
BLACK OR WHITE,
GOOD OR BAD,
POSITIVE OR NEGATIVE—
A LOT OF SPACE
EXISTS IN BETWEEN.

4 DON'T CRY BECAUSE IT'S OVER, SMILE BECAUSE IT HAPPENED

In the ninth grade, I put it out into the universe that I wanted a dog. A week later, I received a call from my uncle.

"Kanwer, I found a puppy for you," he said.

"What's the breed?" I asked excitedly. I had been researching different breeds for a while. Fourteen-year-old me was very particular about the type of dog I wanted.

"I don't know . . . he's black. Let me ask."

I waited until he returned with an answer. "He's a German Shepherd."

"Does he come with any shots?"

"He comes with four legs, that's all I know. Do you want a dog or not?"

"Umm, okay!"

And that's how we got Himmatt. The owners of a gas station near my uncle's home had purchased two very expensive German Shepherd show dogs and used them for security. Those guard dogs hooked up, and Himmatt was born in a litter of what I could only imagine were higher functioning puppies. My cousin, who had joined my uncle to visit the litter, explained that while the other dogs were running around play-fighting with each other, Himmatt sat quietly by himself staring at the floor. My uncle figured he'd be the least of a headache and chose him.

I was excited to get a puppy. I imagined him to be a cute and innocent little guy, but Himmatt was none of the above. He was all black with a little brown on his nose, and he was much larger than I expected an eight-week-old puppy to be.

Himmatt is a Punjabi word that loosely translates to *courage* and *strength*. He was goofy-looking and had oversized paws that he'd trip over as he walked. His ears drooped and never pointed in the same direction. When we were out on a walk together, people would stop their cars to get a closer look and pet him. They'd tell stories of their former dogs as they searched for them in his eyes. At the time I thought these people were weird and creepy, but the more it happened, the more I realized how easily dogs bring smiles into people's lives.

Himmatt grew to be a large and handsome dog. He grew to 140 pounds and could jump and catch something six feet in the air. His show dog parents passed down show dog genes to him. He was a smart guy and knew enough to know when he didn't have to listen. He knew who in my family would share dinner scraps with him. He knew the best routes for walks and would ignore anyone who wasn't going where he wanted to go. He knew when to be nice to little kids and little dogs, and he knew he wasn't allowed on couches, so he waited until we fell asleep to jump on them.

Himmatt grew up with us and was there for both of my sisters' weddings. He had friends and enemies in the neighborhood, could sit on the porch without a leash, and was trustworthy enough to even leave the mailman alone.*

---

* Until he didn't, and we got a ticket from the city that said we had to neuter him.

When he was ten years old, he developed problems in his hips and struggled to walk. We had been warned that this could happen with German Shepherds, but we had hoped we wouldn't have to face this situation. First, he began to walk on only three legs, leaving one of his hind legs up. Then, the second hind leg started to give out as well, leaving him immobile. He would have accidents in the house, and we watched him deteriorate. German Shepherds have a life expectancy of nine to thirteen years, and, by the time he was eleven, the severity of his hip problems no longer allowed him any independence.

Just as I had researched information before getting a dog, I started researching what signs to look for when it was time to let him go. It's extremely difficult to make a decision about another being's life. I read heartbreaking stories from pet owners about their experiences with trying to figure out the "right" time—if that even exists. One person wrote that they asked their dog directly whether it was time, hoping for a sign. They said they felt that their dog gave them permission to let go, but more important, permission to forgive themselves.

Desperate, I began to talk to Himmatt. I asked him whether he thought it was time to go, but I didn't get any type of response. I kept asking him over and over, crying, hoping for anything—a nod, a bark, a whimper, anything. His eyes would widen if I offered him ice cream or asked him whether he wanted to go for a walk. But when I asked him whether he thought he was going to be alright, if we should hold out hope that he remain with us a little longer, he just looked away.

One early morning, my father woke me up and said that Himmatt couldn't get up anymore. He'd had another accident and was struggling to move. My father told me I needed to call the veterinarian and make arrangements.

That call was the heaviest thing I had ever dealt with, and in a painfully symbolic moment, Himmatt found the strength to get up and walk to the backyard while I was calling the vet. I hung up on the receptionist and ran to him. He sat there casually, as if everything was okay. I gave him a hug, and he groaned, letting me know that he wanted his space. Then he struggled to get up again.

I took a picture of him for the last time.

We went to the vet that afternoon, a place he always hated; it made him anxious and turned him—this giant dog—into a big baby. In hindsight I wished I had explored other options, like bringing the vet to the house and releasing Himmatt in a place where he was most comfortable. It still haunts me to see him on the cold steel table, whimpering, looking at me, wondering why I wasn't helping him. I could have made his last moments better; he deserved that much. I failed him there.

When dogs are euthanized, they're first given a drug that puts them to sleep, and then a second drug stops their heart. I hugged him and sobbed as he shook and whimpered.

I'm sorry I'm sorry I'm sorry I'm sorry I love you so much, I'm sorry!

Nothing else would come out, not a "goodbye," not an "I'll miss you," only "I'm sorry."

After the first needle, his whimpers began to fade, and his eyes got heavy. As they began to close, I got one final glimpse into them before the lights went out. He wasn't putting up a struggle anymore, he just lay there, so still and so calm.

When the vet gave him the second drug, I screamed.

I'm sorry I'm sorry I'm sorry I'm sorry!

I buried my face into his and sobbed, his body still warm, fur still soft.

My guy, my buddy, my big dummy, I'm sorry I ever brought you here, I'm sorry you had to go like this!

He was gone.

I'm sorry, I'm sorry!

I spent eleven years with him, and it's been eleven years since he's been gone, and my eyes still well up with tears every time I think of him.*

To this day, I always stop to pet people's dogs, and I tell the owners my stories of Himmatt. I'm always checking the dogs' paws to see how big they'll grow, always staring into their eyes, looking for my big dummy.

Once, I spotted a German Shepherd that looked exactly like Himmatt—so much so that I froze when I saw him, hoping he'd recognize me, hoping he'd come running to me, jumping at me, almost knocking me down every time. It felt too real to even go near him. My eyes filled with tears until I couldn't see him anymore. I wiped away the tears and, as clear as day, I saw Himmatt in his eyes.

I promised myself never to get a dog again. Even if they live long and healthy lives, it's still only a fraction of my own. That's painful to know. Having to say goodbye to Himmatt was one of the hardest things I've ever had to do, and I'm starting to realize why.

Control.

We can't control death; we can manage or delay it, but we can never outright avoid it. Even modern science focuses on lifespan over healthspan, as we create suffering just to avoid the inevitable. The thought of a new dog pushes me to the thought of those last moments, when I'll have to make that decision again one day, to decide that a beloved dog no longer gets to exist.

---

* Even as I'm proofreading this chapter.

Nicht weinen, weil sie vorüber!
Lächeln, weil sie gewesen!
[Do not cry because they are past!
Smile, because they once were!]
—Ludwig Jacobowski

This Dr. Seuss–esque idea has been floating around forever, but clichéd quotations lose meaning if we forget why they are clichés in the first place.

All of our relationships are seasons. Some last longer than others, and even at their best, a relationship will still change and fall. It's our fear of not being in control that makes us bitter and greedy in the face of the truth that everything is temporary . . . including us. It's an inconvenient truth that we never want thrown in our faces, so we do everything and anything to avoid or disguise it. Some chase legacies beyond their years, others lean on science, others on religion. Whatever it may be, all lives play out the same: we will lose others, and others will lose us.

Life is going to be full of tough decisions, and some questions will never have clear answers. Did we put Himmatt down too early? Could he have had a few more days? Who would have benefited from those few days? Did we wait too long? Such questions won't deliver any answers that will bring peace to my mind. It happened, and should I choose to get another dog, it'll happen again. The important question, the one we can answer through our actions is, Was having eleven years with Himmatt worth the pain of losing him?

The answer is an astounding, absolute *yes*. In my unapologetic, biased opinion, there are two types of people: those who love dogs, and those who haven't owned a dog. It was an amazing experience, and like all experiences, it came to an end. The fact that it ended is one of the reasons it was so valuable. I learned responsibility, love, and affection and experienced the magic that is having a four-legged best friend.

Here's why this matters: We will all suffer loss. It's a guarantee in life. Some losses are easier to bear over time; others permanently affect who we are and the direction we move in life. But the pain of loss, much like the pain of anything, is a part of the natural cycle in this beautiful thing called life. Our fears tell us that we should avoid long-term enriching experiences because they may end in loss. But when we give in to those fears, all we do is close ourselves off to an endless well of magic.

I don't know whether I'll be able to open my heart again to a dog. I don't know whether meeting that woman on a blind date will lead to a life-long relationship. I'm unsure whether devoting a year to writing a book is worth it. But fear won't do anything other than hold me back from finding out.

I'm not here to promise you that everything will work out. I don't own a crystal ball. That person you started dating may betray your trust next week, month, year, or fourteen years from now. That puppy you bought may drain your bank account with veterinary bills. Sharing your work with the public may blow up in your face. I'm not here to sell you affirmations. I'm here to remind you that despite all the things that can (and often will) go wrong, it's worth going for it. Holding yourself back from experiencing life will leave stains on your spirit that may never come out.

Of course, sometimes, going for it has negative consequences. But I've always come out the other side. I have tattoos I don't like—so what? I've spent my life savings on projects that failed—so what? I've loved with my eyes closed and was torn to shreds—but I'm still here. More important than my stories of surviving the worst-case scenarios are your stories. You've suffered and will continue to suffer loss, and often it's out of your hands. But you do hold the power of deciding whether you can handle more loss and whether the journey is worth it despite the loss.

I cried writing this chapter because I miss Himmatt with all my heart. A new dog wouldn't replace him; it would only be a new experience and adventure, with its own ups and downs, problems and solutions, beauty and horror. I've given myself permission to be fearful, but I won't allow those feelings of fear to decide my actions moving forward. My fear of loss doesn't have to stop me from having relationships with dogs that my friends' live with or dogs I pass on the street.

For you, fear might mean taking that baby step toward a first date, or even having a conversation with your crush. Maybe it's spending time in a new city, or actively searching out new people to connect with. We don't have control over how 99.999999 percent of things turn out, but we'll always have control over our efforts and our perspectives, and that counts for something. If we go in with an open heart toward the possibility of loss, then maybe the blow won't feel so traumatic. As someone who's NOT Winnie the Pooh once said: "How lucky am I to have something that makes saying goodbye so hard."

All of our emotions have value, and as unpleasant as some are, they're reminders that we're alive and have a whole lot going on inside. Why not approach life with curiosity and wonder, instead of dread and fear. We don't avoid movies because we know they'll end. We enjoy the journey they take us on. Our journey is life, and no one makes it out alive; the finish is death, so let's enjoy life while we can, with those we love, while they're still here.

Eleven years with Himmatt was most definitely better than never having him at all. Every day was a gift, and now being grateful for that gift is my priority. **It's okay to make room for the fear and self-pity; just be mindful that they don't overstay their welcome.**

IT'S OUR FEAR OF NOT
BEING IN CONTROL THAT
MAKES US BITTER AND
GREEDY IN THE FACE OF THE
TRUTH THAT EVERYTHING
IS TEMPORARY . . .
INCLUDING US.

CLOSE

If things lasted forever, would we be able to appreciate them?

I'm writing this while I sit in first class flying to LA from NYC, eating a warm chocolate chip cookie, which was a great follow-up to Dessert Part 1: a hot fudge sundae. This is my first, and maybe last, time flying first class, and no, I didn't pay for this ticket. To get it, all I did was agree to attend an event. I napped, watched a few reruns of *30 Rock*, and ate every piece of food I was offered, because I don't know whether this will ever happen again. I know that the people sitting beside me consider this an average day, and because of that, they don't appreciate it the way I do.

I can appreciate this humble brag only because I've learned that as quick as it comes is as quick as it goes. The fact that nothing lasts forever is a double-edged sword, and we have to be careful. Just because nothing is going to last doesn't mean we can abandon our responsibilities. Statistically speaking, if you're reading this, then the odds are in your favor that you'll be here for a solid three-quarters of a century, and that means you have to plan accordingly. Our circumstances last longer than our feelings, but it's those feelings that have a massive impact on our circumstances. I'm only a kid in a candy store on this flight because I'm aware that this experience is a short, rare one and so I should make the most of it. Most of the wonderful things and people we have in our lives are just like this first-class flight: temporary, rare, and worth our highest levels of gratitude. Letting go is never easy when we get used to things.

This flight won't last forever, and that's important, because if it did, I wouldn't appreciate it. Despite the comforts, extra accommodating flight attendants, and their magical ability to keep the ice cream cold, I wouldn't want this flight to last forever. I want to have other experiences, and those will also come with an expiry date. The challenge is, we want the good stuff to last and struggle to believe that the bad stuff will ever end. The heartbreaks, regrets, pain of loss all seem to tattoo themselves into our beings, but just like this flight, they won't last. **Sometimes the only reason these feelings stick around is because we don't let them go.**

Nothing remains forever, and that idea scares and excites the shit out of me at the same time. It's that rollercoaster of our life in the theme park we built, and it's fun only because it makes us feel butterflies in our tummies. The glory of our victories and the disappointments of our defeats all become memories. When we realize this, we're free to choose dread or gratitude when facing them. Gratitude is the only thing that will make us smile, so if smiling is your jam, lean in that direction.

Everyone wants to avoid the reality of death and how temporary everything is. We're coded to survive, so it makes sense that we have our blockers on; it wouldn't make for much of a life if we viewed everything as simply temporary, and thus not worth our time. But we don't have to choose to see the world one way or the other. Life is a spectrum of experiences, and we can dance in between them, because between is all that matters. Life is what happens between birth and death—that little hyphen that shows up on our gravestones between our birthday and our death day. It's the between that allows me to goof around and get work done on this comfortable six-hour flight. It's that in-between period in life that opens up endless possibilities for what our lives can become.

One day the star we call our sun will burn out, the galaxy we call the Milky Way will fade, the universe we call home will cease to be, and there will be nothing. Before any of that happens, we'll become nothing too, and that's okay; it just means we should appreciate who and what we have, while we have them, for however long we have left.

I hope someone is reading this well after I'm gone and is scratching his or her head about what a first-class flight is.* I'll take comfort in knowing my thoughts outlived the mind that manifested them, if only for a few extra millennia.

---

* I hope that person exists in that sweet spot in time when we're all traveling on beams of light, but still reading books.

Exit

You won't return like the sunrise
But I'll feel your warmth
What did I do to deserve the few moments we had
I'm overwhelmed
When you brought me pain, you brought me rain
And a seed of wisdom came to sprout
Your voice vibrates with a half-life of infinity
Everything will be said, will be said forever
Until there's no one left to hear it
And then it won't matter
In a temporary world, it matters that you shared your temporary
   time with me
I'll see you in forever

KNOWING
YOURSELF
MAKES ALL THE
DIFFERENCE

Enter

Roses are red, violets are blue
Listening to your parents
Means you don't have to decide what to do

Sugar is sweet, syrup is sappy
Stick to the script
and keep everyone happy

Decisions are exhausting, and everybody likes to blame
So don't rock the boat
And you won't have to worry about them

Life is confusing, someone's got to have the answers
And if they're amusing, let's make them our mentor

Let's avoid the mirrors and allow others to paint our pictures
Of who we should be, without ever knowing who we are

The cost of being yourself, is being by yourself
And that's a pretty penny I can't afford

But staying in line has its cost
Keeping everyone else happy but ourselves

OPEN

What do you want to eat?
I don't know, what do you want to eat?
I'm too tired to decide, just pick anything.

Making decisions takes energy, and it gets exhausting. There's a term for this. It's called *decision fatigue*, and it's the reason that Steve Jobs, founder of Apple, always wore the same black turtleneck and blue jeans. It's the reason Jeff Bezos, founder of Amazon, expects himself to make only three good decisions a day. These high-functioning individuals understand the importance of every decision they make and what it takes from them, so they reduce the number of decisions they make. Jobs did it by wearing the same clothes, to avoid that first decision of the day. Bezos understands that he can make only a finite number of good decisions each day, so he aims to make only three.

The rest of us have found our own hacks, like packing our lunch and laying out our clothes for the next day the night before. But in the bigger picture, with the big decisions in life, we're either too overwhelmed with the options or constrained by the rules that society, culture, and friends and family have placed on us. The decisions we can't make with confidence end up being made for us. That's why so many of us are in school studying something we don't like; getting an education is a realistic way to plug ourselves in to society and earn a living, allowing us to feel accepted by everyone else—and also to not embarrass our families.

That template isn't just related to our careers; it's related to our beliefs, values, and pursuits of happiness. Go to school, get a job, get married, have 2.5 kids, put them through school, get them married, have 2.5 grandkids, and retire, wait for death, while you reminisce about how horrible you were at math.

For those few of us who decide to go off-script, we're leaving a zoo to enter the jungle. Sure, there's an abundance of freedom when we choose to go against the template, but with that freedom comes new challenges. We have to trade feelings of safety and security for uncertainty, and we have to learn how to be out on our own. All the decisions that were previously made for us now rest solely on our shoulders.

And that's fucking exhausting.

Many people give up and rejoin the templated life, where the path is so beaten, it's paved with pretty lines and streetlights, which is much nicer than the dark dangerous uncertain jungle. There are fewer decisions to make and more guidelines for how it all works. Hit that benchmark at work by this age. Have kids now. Wait to travel the world.

Sticking to the script saves us from having to make a lot of tough decisions, but tough decisions still find us, often when life doesn't go according to plan. The beauty in those tough decisions is that they teach us about ourselves.

We've been fed messages of how to know ourselves throughout our lives. The corny after-school specials always half-heartedly encouraged us to be ourselves. Social media found a way for us to sell an idea of our authentic selves. But the truth is, we have to go through bullshit in order to learn who we really are. When we get those moments, we realize one simple truth:

You can't be yourself if you don't know who you are.

So how do you know who you are? Everyone is a gooey batter of both nature and nurture, and every time shit hits the fan in our lives, we have an opportunity to get to know ourselves a bit better. It's an exhausting experience, but it's enriching.

We learn about ourselves through all of our interactions with the world, both good and bad. This is the reason your fourth-grade teacher taught you about rocks—not because it's important to know the difference between sedimentary, igneous, and metamorphic rocks, but because a little dabble on a subject may awaken something in you to help you become the next Charles Darwin or Ross Geller.

So with everything you do, think about how it shapes who you are, and think about how who you are shapes your experience of everything you do.

The more you know yourself, the more you can live a life that feels right for you. The life you want to live will rarely be one-size-fits-all. Society, culture, and all the people you care about will try to make decisions for you, accidentally reinforcing their own desires for your conformity. But with conforming comes the kind of stress that can't be meditated away ten minutes a day using an app on your phone.

The journey to know yourself better isn't paved and doesn't come with a map. That's why you often feel like you're lost or broken. Every moment when you've discovered something new about yourself likely happened the hard way, but it was worth it.

There's nothing more important than being self-aware, and although it takes more brainpower than simply falling in line, it'll save you so much more heartache, headache, and tension in the long run. That type of tension is what has us chasing fixes and distractions, avoiding the very inconvenient truth that stares us all in the mirror every day:

I'm not happy where I am right now.

Every promise broken, every heart-breaking moment, and even the random glimpses of hope can teach us about who we are, and what we want. Knowing these things will make all the difference in the life we have, the life we want, and how to bring the two together.

5

WE CAN
SURVIVE A LOT

It was every dweeb's dream—a message from a very pretty girl acknowledging the dweeb's existence: "I know you're the brains behind the operation."

The operation she spoke about was comedy YouTube videos I put out along with a few friends called *Harman The Hater*. I wasn't in the videos, but I directed, edited, and provided color commentary for them. I was a voice behind the camera, known only as *Kman*.

She noticed that, and she noticed me.

And she was gorgeous.

She had the most dangerous eyes, and she spoke with such assertiveness. We'd talk online, and then on the phone. After one long conversation lasting the entire night, we met at 6 a.m. on a dare.

Our second date was at a Christmas party thrown by the elementary school where I was a teacher. She introduced herself to everyone as my fiancée; she was fearless and bold, like Angelina Jolie's character in any movie she's ever done.

By the third date, we had already planned a trip together: Thailand for three weeks. It didn't matter whether either of us was uncomfortable with the idea; we wouldn't dare admit it. We fed each other's rebellious sides. Our families weren't from the same country, language, or faith. Every decision we made had to be an adventure.

She probably got fired from four jobs while we were together, most often for talking back to her superiors. She was very entitled, but stood up for herself, and every time she lost a job, she'd find another—something more interesting and exciting.

For a while, she was working at a small cafe in Toronto that was a front for the illegal gambling machines kept in the back. She was paid cash to serve coffee, but mainly to keep an eye on the special clientele and watch out for cops. She fawned over work stories of simply sitting by the window, reading the newspaper, drinking a cappuccino, kissed by the sun, as regulars greeted her and then headed to the back room to lose money.

We explored the world, life, and ourselves together. She was the first person to tell me "the world needs to hear your ideas," but at the same time, she saw my infancy celebrity as annoying. She didn't want to wait an hour after my shows as I took pictures with fans; it bored her and made her restless.

Our relationship worked when our priorities matched, and that usually centered around our shared desire for adventure, but also the stability of having each other. Our phone conversations lasted for hours, even after a year of dating, because we were both curious about ideas and subjects beyond ourselves.

When I spoke to her in person, she stared at me with those dangerous eyes, scanning my face, twitching her little rodent nose, as if trying to interpret abstract art. She told me I had the most beautiful forehead and that no other girls were allowed to see it.

When we fought, it was intense. She was the first woman I'd ever met who said things she didn't mean when she argued.

"Oh, you fucked up now! This is over! You fucked this up so bad, you're going to regret this for the rest of your life!"

And I would sit there, with tears filling my eyes, trying to figure out how I'd fucked it up so bad. Hours later she would console me and tell me she didn't mean it.

Except the times she did.

People would compliment me on her, as if she were a trophy wife, and I remember not knowing how to reply when someone told me how beautiful she was.

Thanks, she gets it from me.

Thanks, but I think I'm better looking.

Umm . . . thanks.

Obviously! That's why I'm with her!

One dude even told me that he was proud to see a fellow Singh* with such an attractive woman, because it was a "good look."

Although I dismissed a lot of the comments, they affected me, and I began to think I was with someone who was out of my league, and I couldn't do better. Her beauty was intimidating, and it magnified my insecurities.

As our arguments got harder and my list of insecurities got longer, I felt the relationship going downhill. She always noticed me, until she didn't, and the moments she didn't (often on purpose), I would boil in frustration.

Our first breakup broke me.

I stayed in bed for two days, trying to figure out how I could continue existing without her in my life. She was all I knew, and the best part about me. When she left, so did the life I dreamed about, along with my self-worth and any enthusiasm I held for the future. I cried and blamed others for creating a wedge between us. I refused to speak to anyone, while simultaneously soaking up any pity that came

---

* Singh = turban & beard.

my way. News of our breakup spread quickly through the school where I worked, including my pity party reaction to it.

When I got back to work, a colleague sat me down and gave me The Chat: "I'm divorced with two kids, and watching my marriage crumble was the hardest thing I ever had to endure. I'm not the only person at this school who's gone through hardships, and neither are you. But one thing we have to remember is, the world doesn't stop for our tragedies; it keeps moving, and we have to keep moving with it. Stop handling your tragedies like a child, and deal with them like an adult. Adults show up for work, children stay in bed."

Those words didn't affect me immediately, but they were a sleeper cell. It wasn't until after another on-again, off-again drama and we broke up a final time that I started to accept what it meant to "deal with" this.

She had left Toronto to teach English in South Korea, and a few weeks later she messaged me to say things were too heavy and she didn't want to be in a relationship anymore. I didn't crumble in heartbreak like I had so many times in the past. I went to work and had a productive day.

It wasn't easy, but it was necessary. I channeled my frustration over her into my work and let the pain live for a purpose beyond me.

There were still tears, hard nights, and the urge to send her messages, but I didn't let those things affect my day-to-day life this time. I handled it like an adult.

If you had you asked me, even six months before, to think about losing her, I would have contemplated suicide. I had no faith in myself or my ability to move past any heartbreak. What changed when we broke up for the last time? Maybe it was a little of my seeing it coming, a little bit of my understanding that I couldn't do much since she was halfway around the world, and a little bit of my being relieved that the rollercoaster ride was over.

I realized what I was capable of surviving. I'd already experienced so much pain in our numerous other breakups, and I made it through because I took my colleague's advice to take things one day at a time. None of us knows how strong we are until being strong is the only option we have left. We spend so much of our lives avoiding discomfort that we don't realize that in those uncomfortable situations, our best selves emerge.

I had feared for months that I would lose her, but that vision of how bad the breakup would feel existed only in my head. The reality was different. Our worst fears are rarely realized, and even when they are, we're still standing.

Just as there's a day following the good news, there's always a day after the bad news. As my colleague said, **"The world doesn't stop for our tragedies,"** and neither should we. So, when you've cried all you can cry and complained all you can complain, remember there's going to be another day after all of that, and you just have to keep going to see it.

I'd love to tell you that was the end of our story, but with her, there may never be an end. As I got more popular, ironically, I became more of a global citizen than she did, and our paths crossed a few times. We agreed to keep each other company in Bali, I crashed on her couch in Birmingham, she brought friends to watch my show in Dubai; and when I was living in Los Angeles and becoming more of a mainstream character in the world of entertainment, she called me to say, "What the fuck are you doing? You're above this, your purpose is more important than being famous."

She was still loving me from afar.

Years after this love story ran its course,* the lesson that the world

---

* She married a few years back, and halfway through my writing this chapter, she gave birth to her second child, so I heard.

doesn't stop because of our tragedies has saved me. This painful experience showed me that I'm much tougher than I thought and that I should give myself more credit than I do. I have a feeling that applies to you as well.

We can survive a lot. Surviving things in the short term may be very unpleasant, but in the long term, we will gain in character, strength, and wisdom. I've kept that message with me as I face new challenges in life, knowing that no matter what happens, I'll be able to claw myself out of the holes and come out stronger.

Fear keeps us in line, and the moment we realize how much we're capable of enduring, the fences that hold us back start to disintegrate.

The freedom that comes with moving despite the fear is a liberation we would all benefit from.

I'm grateful she and I are on healthy-ish terms; it couldn't have been easy for her to end things when she did, and how she did, and it must have been just as difficult for her to try to come back.

Let's stop avoiding painful situations, because that's where all the growth lives.

After our relationship had faded, and much to the chagrin of her new beaus, she still talked about me and shared my work with people in her life. Girls in my life told me that I was still in love with her, and I laughed and simply said, "It doesn't matter if I am; love isn't enough to put up with her shit." Sometimes it's best to love someone from afar.

Her last message to me was, "Let's revisit this when you're seventy and no other girl wants you." Look out for us—one day we'll be a rebellious cute old couple sitting at the park, up to no good.

FEAR KEEPS US IN LINE,
AND THE MOMENT WE
REALIZE HOW MUCH WE'RE
CAPABLE OF ENDURING,
THE FENCES THAT
HOLD US BACK
START TO DISINTEGRATE.

6

SERVICE TO OTHERS IS ALSO A GREAT SERVICE TO OURSELVES (*SEWA*)

Sewa (n.): Sikh term for service.

Dharmendra is one of the biggest names and most recognizable faces in Bollywood history, and he's Punjabi—like my family. Punjabis make up less than 3 percent of India's population, so when I had a chance encounter with Dharmendra one evening at a film festival, it was like encountering royalty and I knew I had to take a photo with him to send to my parents, who grew up watching his movies.

I sent the picture to my mom, thinking she'd get a kick out of it. Instead, I got a call from her immediately, her voice sounding shocked and upset. "I wanted to see him in real life at that same film festival," she told me, "but your dad didn't want to go."

Score one for married life.

I felt horrible. I hadn't known my mom knew about the festival, let alone wanted to go, and then I'd met her hero by accident and rubbed it in her face. I felt bad and decided to be mindful of how I share memorable moments of my life without triggering whatever version of FOMO Punjabi moms have.

When I told my father, his response was much different from my mother's: "Wow, I'm so proud my son got to meet my hero." He was smiling ear to ear, regaling me with stories about how he and his friends skipped school to watch Dharmendra's movies as teenagers.

"He was never too famous to go back to his village," my father told me. "He would just have to sneak in at night, so no one would notice him, but he would always go back and hang out with his friends. He hasn't changed a bit."

My mother interrupted, "And you won't take me to see him at the festival awards show."

"We should go!" my dad said, the excitement giving him a change of heart.

Inspired by my father's enthusiasm, and feeling like trash for rubbing it in my mom's face, I decided I needed to make this happen. I connected with the friend who had taken me to the event the night before. "Listen man, I'm willing to put my fingerprints on a murder weapon for you—you have to help me get my parents to meet Dharmendra."

After a little bit more poking and persistence, he agreed to try. A few minutes later he called and told me to come with my parents to a hotel in a few hours. I told my mother I had a business meeting with some older Punjabi men and I needed her to come with me to this hotel to translate. At the same time, I called my dad and told him that I was stranded at a hotel and needed a ride home. Neither knew the other was going to be at the hotel.

The wonderful thing about my parents is that whenever I call them for any type of help, small or big, they show up, no matter what. This was a reminder of how sweet they can be—and also how easy it is to trick them.

At the hotel, my mom and dad were surprised to see each other, but that was short-lived as I hit them with the bigger news: we were going to meet Dharmendra!

My mom was speechless, and my dad simply said "No!" and began walking back to his cab. I ran after him asking "What's wrong?" and his only reply was "No" as he tried to get into the cab. I stopped him and again asked what was wrong. He pointed down to his sandals, track pants, and dress shirt and said "I can't go looking like this."

I understand where my dad was coming from. It was both a beautiful moment where I saw his vulnerability, but with the clock ticking, it was more an unnecessary roadblock to a once-in-a-lifetime experience.

I harshly replied, "Dad, this is happening, let's go!"

As we headed up to Dharmendra's suite in the hotel, I caught a glimpse of my father adjusting his shirt in the reflection of the elevator door. I had never seen him so frazzled and adorable at the same time; my heart melted. My mother was simply quiet—a little too quiet.

We knocked on the door, and to our surprise, Dharmendra answered. An even bigger shock was that it was just him and a friend in the suite. He invited my parents in, sat them down, and offered them tea. He was so warm and welcoming to my parents, and very sweet and down to earth, just as my father had described.

They told him the story of how I had surprised them with this encounter, and he praised me for being a good son.[*] What was even more beautiful, and the icing on the cake of the whole experience, was that nobody rushed the moment. Dharmendra was attentive

---

[*] I'm not gonna lie; that's a pretty good co-sign, and I'm holding it in my back pocket in case I get in serious trouble with my folks.

and interested about my parents' villages back home, and his friend seemed to enjoy the reminiscing as well.

We took some pictures,* and then we headed on our way. As we walked out of the hotel lobby, my father said something I didn't even think an immigrant father could ever say, "You made my dream come true."

And I didn't just hear what my father said; I felt it in my chest. I didn't even know this man had dreams. I'm not sure he did either, until this happened. This is important, because seven years later, this still stands as the most memorable moment of my career, if not my life.

As the world progresses, we're going to get opportunities to build upon what people before us created, and because of that, our default days are lived beyond what most of them expected life to be. I was two years into my full-time journey as Humble the Poet, still not making any money and unsure whether I could stick through the tough time, until I helped my parents meet their hero. Hearing my father say those words gave me a feeling that reshaped my purpose and resolve to continue this journey.

We all have a higher need to contribute to things and people beyond ourselves, but so few of us act on that need, let alone recognize it. For me, meeting Dharmendra meant taking a cool picture, but for two kids who grew up in villages that didn't have electricity, there was nothing bigger. Giving this gift to them was also a gift to myself: it gave me perspective, a sense of gratitude, and a reminder of where I came from. I spend the majority of my life pursuing my ambitions and goals, hoping that passing milestones will somehow make me feel better about all the challenges in my life, but it doesn't. Putting my personal priorities to the side and devoting a day to making my

---

* By "some," I mean about a hundred, to be safe.

parents happy provided me with a goal that was not only energizing to work toward, but also felt so much better than anything I had done to simply scratch a selfish itch. Doing for them, and the feelings it gave me, encouraged me to continue doing for others, especially if I wanted to feel good about myself regularly.

I don't think I have any dreams as big as my dad's. I grew up as the youngest child, witnessing my parents' journey from new immigrant to middle class. There are very few things on this planet that I could selfishly enjoy on that level. My parents didn't wake up that morning expecting to have their wildest dreams fulfilled. The immigrant narrative dictated that their dreams should be modest and realistic, which is what they tried to pass down to their kids. I was just the son who decided that "modest" and "realistic" weren't my glass slipper.

The gift this experience gave me was the realization that nothing I do for myself will ever match the feelings that come from doing things for those I care about. My ambitions will always reinforce that what I have isn't enough, and the experiences I have will often feel like mere stepping stones to the next big thing. So in my moments of feeling unfulfilled or, on a basic level, unhappy, I remember that making things happen for the ones who own real estate in my heart always gives me a sense of joy and gratitude.

Remember: We're not chasing the goal, we're chasing the feeling that we THINK will come from hitting the goal. Doing for others will always feel better than doing for ourselves. We'll also realize there's much less resistance and fewer obstacles when we choose to serve others versus when we choose to do things selfishly.

Being a full-time artist is fantastic, but no matter how many amazing gigs I get or people I meet, none of it compares to those six words that came out of my father's mouth:

"You made my dream come true."

This moment taught me that I care about making people feel seen and loved. That I gain a sense of self from that experience. Specifically, it pushed me to think about bigger questions, like what it means to have a wild, unlikely dream. I'm now obsessed with knowing whether these old folks have any more dreams. My father wanted to see Kenya, so we went there.* My mom wants to see Venice and the Great Wall, and both of those trips will happen, too.

We come to points where we think we know our purpose, and even though the impact of the big moment can fizzle or evolve, it makes a lasting impression if we pay attention. **So ask yourself: What did you learn about yourself in those moments when you helped others?** What did you figure out about yourself when you did a favor for a friend or surprised your family with something? How can you use the challenges you have faced to add value to the life of someone else? When was the last time you focused your energy to help someone you cared about? How did that feel?

The day I introduced Dharmendra to my parents, I realized that my purpose was beyond myself. Focusing on making seemingly impossible things happen for those I care about is something that will always get me out of bed and keep me working, even on the toughest days.

Let's focus on what we can do for others and pay attention to how that makes us feel about ourselves. Service may save us from a lifetime of chasing happiness in all the wrong self-absorbed places.

Note: The friend who made this moment happen for us, the one whom I offered to put my fingerprints on a murder weapon for, never asked for a favor in return. He did me this solid back in 2012, and he did it selflessly. Thank you!

---

* Although I realized later that it was really Tanzania he wanted to see.

DOING FOR OTHERS WILL
ALWAYS FEEL BETTER THAN
DOING FOR OURSELVES.

7 WHEN WE KNOW OUR WHY, OUR HOW GETS EASIER

When I started at university, I had no idea what I wanted to study. Really, no idea. In high school, I had read an article on the top-paying jobs: apparently architects made a great living, and so did computer programmers. Maybe that? I wasn't sure. To me, the reason to go to school was to keep my parents happy and find a job.

My first year of university, my advisor recommended that since I had no real direction or interests I should take all my elective courses during the first year. Normally, people spread out the fun classes throughout their four years, but her logic was to do them first, giving me a year to figure out my shit. Ironically, I experienced the exact opposite.

That first year was great—my classes were interesting, and my grades were good. This probably had a lot to do with the fact that I had no friends at school, and my classes were all at night. But by my second year, my social circle grew and my interest in academics shrank. I had an A average during my first year, which then turned to Bs and then Cs by my second year after I found friends, school clubs, parties, and girls.

By my third year, I started skipping classes regularly, and the Bs and Cs fell to Cs and Ds. But I wasn't too worried, because my plan was to figure things out eventually, take the Graduate Management Admission Test, and go for an MBA. A family friend who had done that had two prestigious internships at Ford and Nike. That sounded cool to me, so why not? Besides, at the time, I was doing well for myself as a club promoter, making extra cash by persuading my friends to throw their birthday parties at various clubs, which got me more friends and VIP treatment at all the cool parties.

It became a regular routine: I would show up at the library to study with some classmates for a math test the next morning, only to find myself, afterwards, at another party, and subsequent afterparties, barely making it to class in time to write the test—and fail.

A few of my friends ended up on academic probation. I, on the other hand, was safe, thanks to my high first-year grades. Still, I was three years into a three-year degree with no completion date in sight.

One evening, I was eating dinner at home with my sister, as we watched *Boston Public*, a dramedy about the lives of teachers at the difficult Winslow High in Boston. At some point during the show, I blurted out, "Wow, it must be so cool to be teacher."

My sister replied, "Why don't you become one?"

"Really? Me?"

"Why not? You'd make a great teacher. You grew up attending all those camps, and you're so good with kids."

I grew up attending youth camps, and by age sixteen, I was facilitating them. But the idea of teaching had never crossed my mind.

She recommended I talk to a friend who was working as an elementary school teacher. I visited him in his classroom one evening, and he sold the entire lifestyle to me in an hour.

This job is so much fun.

No two days are alike.

The money's pretty good.*

If you don't like the classroom, just become a gym teacher.

The hours aren't long.

The benefits are great.

You have plenty of time to do a side hustle if you want.

You really work only nine months a year, with two months off in the summer, Christmas break, March break, and other random long weekends and P.A. days.

The ladies love a guy who teaches, especially those who teach elementary.

He spoke about the promise these young kids held, recounting stories of a refugee Afghani student he had in the second grade whom he helped acclimate to Canadian society.

I was in love. Not only was this a space I was actually interested in, it also didn't seem like too much work to attain. One additional year of university and I would get another degree; two degrees in five years didn't seem so bad. What I didn't know at the time was how competitive Canadian teachers' colleges were. They had a higher rejection rate than some medical schools, as the application numbers far outweighed the spots the schools had.

But for me, things were different: I actually cared about something. With the excitement of this new opportunity, coupled with an ignorance of all the hurdles, I dove headfirst into the application process. The deadline was a month away, and what normally takes a few months to complete, I finished with a week to spare. And I was accepted.

Armed with this new goal to become a teacher, I began to attend classes regularly, as well as the additional tutorials. My fourth

---

* Mind you, I'm Canadian.

year of university was the first time I learned how to study—mapping out chapters, making a plan, and reviewing regularly. It was shocking how well I did on tests and exams. The rust had been shaken off my brain after applying some effort, and I ended up getting As in all my classes—the same math-based programming classes that I had struggled with the year before. Only one thing had changed: I had a purpose.

When I finally became an elementary school teacher, I was thrilled. I'd made it happen. Though the romance of being a teacher didn't last long,* I'd realized how much it mattered to care about something.

I had always been capable, but without motivation ability didn't matter. I'd gone to university with the pragmatic goal of helping me find a job, which would have made my parents happy, but it wasn't enough to keep me going. When I discovered elementary education, my excitement in school was rekindled, which pushed me into action. Moreover, that discovery provided me with an opportunity to be a lifelong learner again. This has stuck with me through my journey to becoming Humble The Poet: I made progress only after I decided my purpose.

> He who has a why to live can bear almost any how.
> —Friedrich Nietzsche, *Twilight of the Idols*

We can debate forever about whether our purpose is given or chosen in life. Personally, I don't think that debate matters as much as identifying what that purpose is. As we get older, it gets more and

---

* My friend forgot to tell me about the vast amount of energy it takes to work with kids; the drain of office politics, continual labor disputes, and combative parents; and the earning ceiling.

more difficult to find people who speak about anything with their eyes wide and full of life. When we find people talking about things that excite them, we become filled with the same enthusiasm.

I'm not going to promise you that discovering your WHY will instantly energize you for the rest of your days. Unpacking our purpose and discovering why the things that excite us do so is a process. The prospect of becoming an educator got me back on track in school and allowed me to bear any challenge to get where I wanted to be. Then my interests changed, and when my energy and enthusiasm for teaching were slowly sapped out, I started to chase another shiny purpose: becoming an artist.

Our purpose can change, and that's okay. The WHY isn't always a fixed thing. Our job is to know ourselves better every day so we can identify the WHY to better equip ourselves to deal with any HOW.

When we find a direction we're enthusiastic about, we don't have to rely on motivational sayings to keep us moving; the journey itself naturally becomes the reward. When we're doing what feels right, it doesn't feel like work. It takes us back to our childhood.

> It is a commonplace among artists and children at
> play that they're not aware of the time or solitude
> while they're chasing their vision.
> —Steven Pressfield, *The War of Art*

Society, religion, and shitty self-help books all have opinions on what our purpose should be, but none of those voices matter if they don't agree with what we're already feeling inside. The more deeply we dive inward, the more clarity we'll have about what tickles our fancy, and we'll quickly realize that purpose is not one-size-fits-all.

We're all capable of more than simply flying by the seat of our pants and spending calories on what we think is important but really may just be urgent. Finding out what's important to us may be the most vital thing we ever do, but that process will always start with knowing ourselves.

I was inspired by watching a television show, but it was also my sister's comment and recommendation that started me on my path. Who knows where I would be if it had not played out that way? As time goes by, I want to continually polish and refine my WHY so I'm not overly bogged down by the HOW. This isn't to say that everything in life can be a pleasant, inspiring, effortless journey of fulfilling our chosen or discovered purpose. Sometimes the work has to get done, and it's not sexy—it's just work, and that's a very real part of life. Let's just ensure that it's not the *only* part of life.

Go out there, try new experiences, and see what connects with you. A whole new life may be waiting for you.

And while you're at it, go inward; relive parts of your life to see whether there's been a pattern to the things you've always gravitated toward. Move beyond your passions to explore your obsessions. Discovering those obsessions will increase the fragments of fulfillment you get to experience on this journey called life.

FINDING OUT WHAT'S
IMPORTANT TO US
MAY BE THE MOST VITAL
THING WE EVER DO,
BUT THAT PROCESS WILL
ALWAYS START WITH
KNOWING OURSELVES.

8

WE GOTTA PAY TUITION FOR LIFE LESSONS

The first car I drove cost me $800. No, I wasn't born a hundred years ago—it was just a twelve-year-old Plymouth Sundance that turned off by itself when I pulled up to intersections. I needed it for university and my part-time job as a telephone market researcher. The job was great for nineteen-year-old me: I got paid a bit more than minimum wage, and the office was right beside my school, so I got free parking.

One rainy afternoon I was driving home from work a bit faster than I should have. As I hit the brakes at a light, the car began to slide. I didn't know what to do, so I panicked and stepped on the brake harder, trying to turn the wheel to avoid the car in front of me. My efforts were futile, and I slid right into a car that was stopped at the red light in front of me.

Holy crap this can't be happening!

I got out of my car and went to check on the driver of the car I had just hit. It was a woman, and her son was in the back seat. He was quiet, and she seemed a bit out of it.

"I'm so sorry, I just kept sliding, are you okay?"

At the moment, she was more interested in her son than speaking to me, understandably, and luckily he didn't seem hurt. Then she turned her attention to me, and with a look of annoyance on her face replied, "It's okay!"

In a panic I continued to apologize. I had never been in a car accident before, and although it wasn't severe and no one was hurt, I was very afraid. I offered to call the police, and she declined, saying she just wanted to get her son home. Neither car showed any damage, and I didn't know what else to do, so I gave her my information and she went on her way. The rest of that trip home I was shaking in fear.

What if she's hurt and just doesn't know it?

What are Mom and Dad going to say when they find out?

What's going to happen to my car insurance?

I went home and spilled the beans. This wasn't a secret I wanted to live with, and I honestly had no idea how to proceed. When my sister heard the story, she immediately said, "You should never admit it's your fault! Now our insurance will go up!"

I didn't understand how car insurance worked, and not only did I feel like a bad person for hitting someone's car with mine, I also felt like an idiot for how I handled it.

The next day we got a call from the husband of the lady I hit. My sister spoke to him, and he seemed very worried. He said his wife had to get stitches from a cut on her forehead and that there was significant damage to the car, neither of which I had noticed at the time; but maybe I was in shock and hadn't seen. I took the phone and apologized profusely. He didn't seem interested in my apologies and kept asking, "Well, how are we going to deal with this now?"

Nobody in my family had ever had to deal with a situation like this before. When I asked how much damage was done to the car, he vaguely replied "a lot." When I asked how much repairs were going to cost, he said it would be more than $2,000. I didn't have $2,000; my life savings were just barely more than $1,000. He said he was going to need money to cover all the damage or we would have to report the accident to insurance. We spoke with our insurance company, and they said they could take care of it, but if they did, they would hike up our premium in the future. It wasn't fair to mess up my family's insurance over my stupidity, so I told the man I could pay $1,000, and he quickly accepted.

A few days later, I took a certified check to the woman whose car I had hit. I was very apologetic, and again she didn't seem very interested in speaking to me. She took the check quickly and said, "It's okay, accidents happen," and told me she had to get back to work. I didn't notice any stitches on her head.

I was devastated watching my bank account depleted to nothing, especially because of what I eventually realized was a scam. Yet looking back at it now, I see that $1,000 as the tuition fee for the school of life.

What did that $1,000 pay for?

It paid for the realization that I, as much as I hate to admit it, am a bit of a romantic and I want to see the best in people. This is obviously good at times, and not so good at others. The car accident was one of those times when it wasn't so good—the $1,000 was a great reminder that being nice and honest doesn't mean everyone else will reciprocate. Although the accident was my fault, in hindsight, I know I didn't cause any damage worth $1,000, and she hadn't been injured. I was scared, and that was exploited. Fear is an easy thing to exploit, and a grown couple with a child had no problem taking advantage of a teenager who just wanted to do the right thing. I always expected that if I was open and honest, others would be open and honest back, but that's not how life works. That $1,000 was well spent because it taught me that lesson, and it was one of many more I'd get throughout my life.

That $1,000 also paid for my first experience of adult accountability. I had fucked up, and I had to respect the causality of my decisions. I've never been in a car accident since, and much of that has to do with my being humbled* by that experience. I learned to pump the breaks on slippery roads and to be mindful of road conditions when I'm driving. We hear the slogan *Arrive Alive* all the time, but this experience hammered that message in, and that's worth more than a grand. It hurt to lose the money, but I also believe I handled the situation like an adult and didn't turn to anyone else to bail me out. We're better off learning early that the cavalry is not coming, and we are responsible for the problems in our lives, whether they are our fault or not. Finger-pointing won't save us from having to fulfill our responsibilities.

The cost of figuring life out can be pricey. Sometimes shit happens, and the best we can do is call it an entrance fee to the amusement park of life.

Finally, I learned it's better not to react prematurely; instead, give things time. The accident was a new experience for me, and I panicked and was taken advantage of. This experience further primed me to slow down my reactions and not dig myself into deeper holes by acting too quickly.

It's one thing for accidents to happen, but how we address them is another thing. I'm grateful this experience happened earlier in my life and I was able to recover from the losses I experienced from it. The wisdom I gained going through it ended up being worth much more than that $1,000.

---

* Pun intended.

To live is to deal with challenges and setbacks. No one is immune to the bullshit life flings our way; but our actions can make that bullshit better or worse. If you look back at your life, the biggest lessons you learned didn't come from a Tumblr quote or celebrity PSA; they came from harsh reality checks when the shit hit the fan. That process isn't going to get any more enjoyable as you grow, but if you anticipate the learning, then the moments you have in life end up being that much more enriched.

Sometimes when the wheels fall off in life, we react in ways that only make things worse. That can start a journey into a downward spiral, or what so many consider "bad luck." Although we don't have control over what happens to us in life, we have control over how we approach the things that happen to us and how much effort we give them. **We have the power to learn from all the mishaps and missteps, and when we look back, we can value them as teachers instead of experience them as regrets.** This has been our story since the first time we touched a hot stove, stuck a fork in a toaster, or put our tongues on a piece of metal on a cold winter day. We live and learn, and the discomfort that comes in that learning is the tuition we pay.

I got a few good years from the Sundance before it took its last spin. It survived a few winters and allowed me to explore the city beyond what I could do taking the bus. It was ironic that a car that cost me $800 cost me another $1,000 after an accident, but I'm still grateful for the time we had together. You never forget your first.

TO LIVE IS TO DEAL WITH
CHALLENGES AND SETBACKS.
NO ONE IS IMMUNE
TO THE BULLSHIT
LIFE FLINGS OUR WAY;
BUT OUR ACTIONS CAN
MAKE THAT BULLSHIT
BETTER OR WORSE.

CLOSE

We're a work in progress, and I'm not sure what the ratio is between creating ourselves and discovering ourselves, but I'm very certain that the more we explore, experiment, examine, and extract from ourselves, the better off we'll be on this journey called life.

Self-awareness isn't a golden ticket to happiness. If anything, the more we learn about ourselves, the farther we may find ourselves from the rest of the world. When we have a deeper understanding of ourselves and begin to pave our own road, there won't be any traffic, but we also won't have much company. That's often the price of walking to the beat of our own drum: loneliness. Often, that loneliness made me wish I could go back to the days when I believed in the romance and promises life presented me. Back to the days when I could drown out any independent thought, enjoy the trending topics, and feel a part of, and connected to, everyone else. Back to the days when I felt normal.

It sounds comforting, joining the herd, not asking too many questions, and spending our days feeling only inches away from a "happily ever after" that never seems to come. It feels nice to belong, and for tens of thousands of years humans have been living in tribes and finding value and significance in them. Why ruin that all with some self-awareness and the inevitable loneliness that may follow?

Well, that loneliness can be quelled quickly as we develop the most important relationship we have in our lives: the one with ourselves. Leaving the pack and going off script may reduce the number of people we have around us and limit the number of activities we participate in with others, but it'll save us years of spinning our wheels finding no fulfillment in a cookie-cutter life.

People every day choose the red pill and embrace the discomforts that come with straying from the norm. Spending time with other people who devote their lives to self-discovery will only enhance how far you can take your journey. **We are a vast and endless universe.**

I'll never disrespect you and promise you everlasting happiness, or even comfort, when you shift your perspective away from the usual path. It's going to suck, but do push-ups, flossing, or any other activity that's essential to improving the way you feel about life.

When you think about the people you admire the most, and the ones you know the most about, you'll usually find that those are the people you think are cool. "Cool" is simply someone who's comfortable in their own skin. The only way to be that comfortable is by being yourself. The only way to be that unapologetically authentic is by having an ever-improving clarity about who you are, what you want to do, and how that relates to the world around you.

Writing this book is one of the scariest things I've ever done in my life, but it's also been one of the most cathartic and educating. I have learned that sharing my story helps me understand myself and helps others write stories of their own. Through this, we can form communities and grow alongside one another. Sure, as your adventures in discovering and crafting yourself continue, you'll encounter resistance from those around you, but that's okay; some of them will come around, others won't—that's a pattern in life you're better off recognizing earlier than later.

Let's all aim to be cooler people and encourage others to do the same. Not in hopes that we will all fit in, but to celebrate the things that make us all stand out.

Exit

I had to be forgiven to forgive
Forget forgiving myself
A few more winters I had to live

Before I could spot my motif
And take hints at my design
More moons would pass
Before I could decipher a line

Of code, tells my fate
Our histories do rhyme
Our wires stay crossed
Our stories part defined

Sometimes I create, sometimes I find
Myself on the journey
Myself in my mind

Aware more than humble
Aware more than woke
Aware of what I am
Means I don't have to pretend

DON'T FOCUS ON THE POT OF GOLD, ENJOY THE RAINBOW

Enter

Only one more fight and we'll get there
Only one more kiss and we'll get there
Only one more breath and we'll get there
Only one more step and we'll get there
A world with no wants
No problems, no bullshit, no more tight muscles and knots in the
    heart
No more deep sighs and temple rubs,
No more long brokens with short fixes
Only one more
Day of struggle and my chest can poke out again
Like on that jungle gym
Skipping monkey bars
Earning scars
Only one more W, and I can afford the W
Earn their silence, their hate is violent
The milestones are farther than a mile
Good news tonight is forgotten by tomorrow
But only one more
Promise that one more will be enough
If this don't work out, I'm fucked
Only one more fail, and I'm letting go
Too many maybe-next-time's
Maybe next time should be the last
Only one more

OPEN

We've all heard it a million times, "Focus on the journey and not the destination," and once we've hit the millionth time, the saying has already lost all meaning. Have you ever noticed, though, that when you're having fun, you're more present and willing to dig in when you don't have the destination in view? When our teachers were sharing the sounds of the alphabet in kindergarten, we didn't know they were preparing us to read books like the one you're holding. We were just having fun, making funny sounds.

By the time we got to high school, it was clear that we needed to be working toward something for the rest of our lives, and the stress started kicking in. If you wanted to go to college or university, your grades mattered. If you wanted to be financially stable, the money you saved up from that part-time job mattered. A lot more suddenly mattered. Anyone who wasn't planning for the future was considered to be flying by the seat of their pants, living in chaos, doomed to a career quickly rendered obsolete by artificial intelligence.

For most people, it's difficult to enjoy the journey, let alone continue on it, unless we can set our eyes on the finish line. Graduation, the weekend, payday, retirement—we're always working toward something to keep us going; otherwise, why would we do it?

But let's come back to learning the alphabet in kindergarten: Yes, it might have been hard at the time, but five-year-old you probably enjoyed it for the most part. Once you were reading things on your own, you were probably pretty excited about it. Street signs, maybe restaurant menus, then short books. You enjoyed each of those things for what they were, not as building blocks for reading *War and Peace.*

So how do you get to that place now as an adult? How do you enjoy things for what they are, instead of what they are supposed to produce in the end?

I'd be lying if I said this book didn't have an end goal. I'm not just writing for the sake of writing and hitting "print" whenever I feel good.** This time, I have structured milestones and an outline, with regular thoughts of holding this baby in my hand once it's done. It helps when I'm in the middle of a story and hit a wall, and the voices in my head question whether anyone will even care to read this. The pot of gold doesn't have to be the enemy—it's a great motivator. But the key is realizing it can't be the main motivator. That so-called end is often far away and abstract, and we may not recognize it when we hit it.

The challenge is that the older we get, the vaguer our goals become. Maybe it's because we have to set them ourselves. We want to be financially secure, but we've defined that either by playing the comparing game or coming up with an arbitrary milestone like making our "first million." Even more, we think we'll experience a certain feeling when we hit our goal, but the feeling rarely lives up to expectations. You'll make your first million when you aim to make ten, so by the time you hit it, you'll feel only one-tenth of the way there. To make ten, you'll need to aim for a hundred, and so forth.

---

* Why do *g* and *j* sometimes sound the same?
** Although that's how I wrote my first book, *Unlearn*, but my editors wouldn't let that fly this time.

The times we hit that pot of gold, and all our hard work has paid off, we enjoy a few moments of satisfaction and celebration before waking up the next morning and asking ourselves, "What's next?" I don't need to tell you any of this; you experienced it after finishing high school, getting that job you really wanted, or finally being able to move out of your parents' home. There's a great feeling, but it's fleeting, and we're left to create a new goal, in hopes that it will finally bring us the "happily ever after" we long for so much.

But there is no happily ever after, and the pot of gold will never be shiny and satisfying enough to keep us going, so the best we can do is have fun along the way. That means we have to figure out which journeys we'll enjoy the most and not depend on the destination to bring us lasting happiness. **We have to be okay knowing that our journey is ours, and ours alone, and if need be, we may need to abandon one rainbow to have an adventure on another.**

Focusing on the rainbow instead of the pot of gold isn't just one of many philosophies we can adapt—it's the most sustainable way for us to keep going. The present is all we have, and we can promise ourselves only so much contentment before we realize that the story doesn't end until we take our last breath. Once we accept that, we can enjoy the journey, celebrating every baby step we take, not toward a treasure on a map, but in a direction that steadily improves the way we feel about ourselves, our lives, and the world around us.

It's worth noting that Western society is based on Abrahamic theology: Christianity, Judaism, and Islam. All of these traditions focus on life as a straight line with an end goal, whether that's heaven, Jannah, the Second Coming, or the end of the world. So there's a reason you have an end-focused worldview.

Meanwhile, Eastern philosophies such as Sikhi, Hinduism, and Buddhism offer a cyclical perspective. Like the seasons, things start, end, and start again. Just like our lives, old problems solved will create new problems. The life cycle shows how life and death aren't on two ends of a spectrum but rather are part of the same cycle, depending on each other to keep things moving. Our life, as we understand it, has a beginning, middle, and end, but between those are constant cycles. Finding the happy medium between the two will help us manage our expectations of life and embrace the inevitable challenges that come as we continue our journey. We can gain from looking at the world through this lens of Eastern philosophy—beyond just wearing cute yoga pants and mispronouncing *Namaste*. It'll help us recognize the cycles in our lives and to focus less on an end goal that will never come.

Knowing what the journey holds, and still making that journey with enthusiasm, is the real reward life presents, and although we need some direction as to where we're going, let's not overpromise how great arriving at our destination will feel—because we may never arrive.

And that's okay.

9 FOCUS ON THE FUN, AND EVERYTHING ELSE WILL FALL INTO PLACE

(AND IF IT DOESN'T, AT LEAST YOU'RE HAVING FUN)

No pain, no gain.
The hustle never stops.
Sleep when you're dead.
Work harder than hard.
Sleep is for the weak.
By any means necessary.

That mindset is sustainable only with some help. Los Angeles is a magical sunny place full of palm trees, sunshine, and coping mechanisms. The sober guys take Adderall. The young ones who haven't tasted coffee do the energy drinks. The agents sip on overpriced drinks at noon, paid for by their companies. I'm proud to say in the four years I've been doing this city regularly, cocaine hasn't crossed my path, but that's probably because I've been lucky enough to hang out with folks who work more than party.

There are a lot of fake things in Hollywood, but work ethic isn't one of them. The beautiful weather remains, but the laid-back California attitude got pushed out of this city a long time ago. I thought it was the greatest thing. So many hard-working people, in so many different fields, feeding off all their energy and consistency. I wanted to be just like them—how else would I become successful?

I had been Humble the Poet full time for about three years, staying afloat by living a very simple life. That included living in Lilly Singh's spare room in mid-Wilshire, an up-and-coming neighborhood in LA. Los Angeles is where creativity and commerce held hands, and I desperately wanted to begin earning a respectable living off my ideas. I was being exposed to so many people who had accomplished just that, and the common thread I saw among all of them was the steady amount of work they put out into the world.

I would force myself to hit certain daily writing goals: one thousand words, sixteen bars, five pages. Anything with a finish line I could reach so I could feel I'd accomplished something. It wasn't inspiring. It wasn't making me a better writer. It felt more like eating my vegetables because my parents weren't going to let me leave the table until I did. It sucked, and it was taking a toll on me. The toll became so expensive that I found myself procrastinating more and more and even considered going back to my job as a teacher, because I felt so burned out.

I would go for long walks and immediately feel guilty when I got back to Lilly's apartment, seeing her burning the candle on both ends, starting her day before me and finishing after. She did more work in an afternoon than I did in three weeks, and I was desperate to catch up. The thing I failed to realize about Lilly at the time was that she wasn't just a workaholic with the stuff that pays her; she puts 190 percent into everything she does, including the dinner parties she throws.

So it was no surprise when I arrived back in LA to find the closet completely filled with a giant Ping-Pong table.

"Where did this come from?" I asked, already knowing the answer.

"I threw a party while you were away and we needed a Ping-Pong table."

That Ping-Pong table sat in the closet and was never used until Lilly moved into a house a few years later. There, it served as a prop table, dinner table, seat, and sometimes Ping-Pong table.

It wasn't a particularly nice Ping-Pong table. Lilly had grabbed it at Target for less than it would have cost to buy some decent paddles. We didn't even know the rules of the game, but we quickly realized that two games of Ping-Pong woke us up better than any caffeinated beverage ever could, and without the crash or gross feeling. So we found ourselves playing all the time.

Renata, aka Nata, one of Lilly's reps at the time, joined in on the fun. She got really into it, downloading a whistle app on her phone to be a referee and purchasing a scoreboard so we could keep track. We played every day, scheduled it into work breaks, and even began to film the games so we could share the entertaining trash talk with Lilly's community Team Super.

Each of us had our strengths and weakness. The harder you hit the ball at Nata, the easier she could return it. She had a killer back-hand, but her forehand needed work, so I always sent the ball over there. Lilly had an impeccable defense and returned everything you shot at her. But she would get really excited if you hit the ball up high, setting her up to smash it down. Unfortunately, her power and accuracy didn't match, and she often missed the table. I loved everything about the Ping-Pong table—watching people play and playing on my own. When no one was home, I would push the table to the wall and play against myself, or practice trick shots I saw online.

The months flew by, and the table began to sink in the middle. We worked around it. Fans would gift us custom paddles, and we'd play with them, finding what worked and what didn't. Getting in a few games wouldn't take longer than twenty to twenty-five mins, and everyone was always down to play.

Slowly the house got more furniture, and we threw together a little housewarming party. As guests arrived, many noticed the table and declared their skills, challenging the room. As the resident champ, I accepted any and all challenges. I beat everyone I played, not decisively, but enough to even surprise myself.

How did I get so good? I never practiced a day in my life.

That was the moment it hit me. I had been playing regularly for almost a year at that point, and those baby steps had added up and made me a good player.

I required no motivation to play. I didn't have to give myself a pep talk to push the table against the wall, no one made me go deep analyzing my opponents; I chose to do all that. Why? Because it was fun. I didn't worry about chasing anything or hitting any goals; I focused on the fun, and great things happened because of it.

During that year, I didn't consider playing Ping-Pong to be work; it was more a way of procrastinating than anything. I wasn't training to play a tournament. I just played and wanted to get better because it was fun. Over time, Ping-Pong took up more real estate in my brain, but only because I enjoyed it and had no obligation to play.

During this year of accidentally honing my Ping-Pong game, I'd been struggling professionally to find the energy to sit down and write. I had to create incentives for myself, give myself pep talks, and resort to caffeine—one of the world's most addictive yet socially accepted drugs. My days were full of avoiding the discomfort of work and pushing myself to break through my procrastination when I did finally sit down to get started.

The difference with Ping-Pong was that playing was its own reward, the challenges made it even more fun, and the tiny progress I was making made me want to keep going—all the while feeling super excited and energized about the process of learning.

I didn't compare myself to better Ping-Pong players or feel like giving up. Better players inspired me to want to be better myself. This was different from my usual pattern of comparing myself to another artist or creator or seeing a carefully crafted life on social media and reassessing my own work and life and always feeling like I was coming up short.

Ping-Pong showed me a different way of approaching life, my work, and my ambitions—an approach that I was very familiar with, far before I had a paddle and table.

That way is to focus on the fun.

How did I get to that place in my work where it wasn't fun anymore? When I first started as an artist, there was no plan to release my stuff: no counting views, money, likes, or accolades. There was only fun. I spent hours after my day job as a teacher writing, recording, editing, revising, rewriting, and rerecording, with no reward on the horizon. Doing the work was fun, and it was only after I tasted some success that fun was replaced with pressure, overthinking, and obligation.

Confucius once said, "Choose a job you love, and you will never have to work a day in your life," but that's a lie. I get to travel the world, have adventures, and write about them, and a lot of it feels like work, much harder work than I ever did when I was a teacher.

You know what else is hard? Trying to return one of Nata's deadly backhands. I spent many frustrating days trying to crack her code, and I eventually did. I worked hard at that, but it was fun.

So, let me update Confucius's quote:

Choose the fun. Don't focus on the love with the hope that it sustains your enthusiasm. When the fun is the focus, the work is the reward. So enjoy the moments of blood, sweat, and tears, or find something else to do. —Humble the Poet*

I realized I needed to make work fun again. I spent a lot of time sitting quietly, trying to reconnect with young Humble, the guy who worked two jobs and still found four hours to work on his music every day. To this day, I still have to dig deep every once in a while to get that extra mile in, but the fun is still the main theme. **When I spend too much time on process and not enough time on content, work stops being fun.** Now, I write because I have things to say instead of finding things to say because I have to write. I remind myself that like Ping-Pong, the challenges aren't supposed to make me sigh, but rather to excite me. They say "Trust the process," but the process doesn't need to be trusted, just enjoyed. The rest will take care of itself.

Making this change paid off. As I focused on the fun and the therapy of writing again, my audience grew because they connected with my authenticity. It was scary at first to slow down my output, but in the long run, it paid off much more than my previous days of prioritizing the quantity of my output over the quality. Having fun and enjoying the journey brought other rewards, and many of them I never would have aimed for. Some of my "least successful" projects have opened the most doors and created great relationships with people who are helping me grow even more. When I was slaving away and measuring my success only in views, likes, and money, I couldn't see those other doors, or even consider connecting with other people. How we measure success can blind us to other treasures.

---

* Feel free to tattoo this saying on your chest, neck, or calf. Forearm tattoos are a bit stale now.

All the inspirational quotes about hustling hard and pushing one-self beyond one's limits have disappeared from my walls and from my life. When speaking to friends and hearing about all the amazingly massive things they're doing, I always reply by asking, "But are you having fun?" The responses are a mix of yes and no, but the question stops everyone in their tracks and gets them thinking.

There's no fun waiting for us after the work; there's just more work. More year-ends, more midterms, more tests, more projects, more patients, more students, more clients, more customers; it never ends, so the least we can do is enjoy it while we're doing it. That can come from either finding something we already enjoy or reprogram-ming what we're already doing to add more fun to it.

I'm not promising a fatter bank account when you focus on the fun; I'm just promising more fun—the type of fun that first made us fall in love with the art we do, before real life soiled it with obliga-tions and commerce. Ping-Pong will forever be a treat for me, and a reminder that I will always have the power to infuse my life and my work with more fun. And like love, the more fun you share, the more fun finds you.

Maybe if we all had a little more fun, we'd need less Adderall, alcohol, caffeine, cocaine, or whatever other tools folks use to keep themselves afloat in such demanding environments. As Lilly got more successful, she designed an ecosystem around fun as well, which has fueled her meteoric rise. I realized she was able to work late be-cause she was having just as much fun writing that script as she was sticking eyeballs into cupcakes for Halloween.

We can all infuse our lives with more fun, whether it's freestyling in the shower or painting portraits no one will ever see. Whatever it is, just remember, if you don't bring the fun into your life, don't expect the fun to find you.

CHOOSE THE FUN.
DON'T FOCUS ON THE LOVE
WITH THE HOPE THAT IT
SUSTAINS YOUR ENTHUSIASM.
WHEN THE FUN IS THE
FOCUS, THE WORK IS THE
REWARD. SO ENJOY THE
MOMENTS OF BLOOD, SWEAT,
AND TEARS, OR FIND
SOMETHING ELSE TO DO.

10 THE POT OF GOLD RARELY MAKES THE JOURNEY WORTH IT

Early in my career as a rapper, I decided to try something completely different: I started booking my own shows. I had just quit my day job as an elementary school teacher and realized, to put it plainly, I needed to make more money. No one was around to show me how to do it, or to do it for me, so I did it all myself.

I jumped right in with some basic marketing and crowdsourcing, and I put a message up online and asked people what cities they wanted to see me in. My following was small but loyal, and at this point, I had performed in only a handful of cities and university campuses in Canada. I was waiting for an invite to New York and London, but they never came. I couldn't wait any longer for people to bring me opportunities, so I began to create them on my own. Fortunately, once I put out the call, all you handsome friends answered and helped me pre-sell tickets and set up my first batch of shows in major cities around the world.

I started with cities where I had friends and asked them to help me find venues where I could perform. Anything that held at least fifty people. Since I was just starting out and was doing it without a label or manager, I had to be innovative. I would make a deal with the venue that they could keep the money at the bar, while I got the ticket sales. Selling fifty tickets at $15 a head is $750, minus equipment rentals and the plane ticket, and I was still coming up short.

So after a few of those shows, I began to sell sponsorships, plastering my sponsors' logos all over my promotions online and even printing them on the free posters I signed and gave to attendees. In addition to that, I sold copies of my first book at the shows. I was using an independent print service and had the books shipped directly to wherever I was performing. I even included a book package when I sold tickets that allowed me to guesstimate how many people wanted the book ahead of time so I wasn't left with too many extras.

Polishing this science of the live show took more than a year, but it was working: I was making more money than I spent. But it took more than three weeks to plan a show. Creating artwork, pushing promotions, negotiating with venues, booking equipment, and the endless slew of logistical issues that needed to be addressed took a lot of time. I spent more time figuring things out and planning much more in the long term to make the shows more cost effective.

And then came London. I'd finally landed a gig in one of the cities I'd dreamed about. I spent three months putting together the show—at a sold-out venue of more than two hundred people. I got a law firm and a charity to generously sponsor the event. I had a box of signed books shipped ahead of time. I did some TV and radio interviews and even had some UK artists ready to join me on the stage. Everyone showed up, and everyone played their part—except for one person: me.

I spent so much time putting the show together that I didn't spend enough time creating or rehearsing a good performance. One media personality walked out of the show during the first five mins tweeting: "Didn't want my first Humble the Poet experience to be with that shitty sound system they have here, I'll wait until he finds a better venue."

But he was wrong; it wasn't the sound, it was me.

I was exhausted, unrehearsed, and absent-minded, and I knew it. I don't think anyone else there would call it a bad night, but I knew it was, because I could have done better. I was stuck in the motions of trying to earn money. I had stopped focusing on what got me to that point: my art.

I had daydreamed about being a full-time artist forever, and here I was spending more time in front of a computer doing everything except art. At that moment I realized that getting paid didn't feel better than doing something that made me happy. That's ironic, because I thought I had learned that lesson when I left teaching to become an artist in the first place. But at some point, everything had stopped being about the adventure and creativity and had become about earning money. I relied on the shows to make money since otherwise I was broke, but it was killing everything else I cared about.

Despite my thin pockets, that moment made me stop booking shows. And because I wasn't earning from shows anymore, I had to downgrade my lifestyle. It was a very welcome trade because it freed up my time so I could create again.

Time is always worth more than money. You can make your money back. But once time is spent, it's gone for good.

I finally put my well-being above my bank account, which had been the end goal that ended up derailing me. I focused on creating and found joy in all the challenges that came with it. Ideas that had been swimming in my brain finally got to see the light of day.

One of the priorities for everything I worked on was that it had to be enjoyable and inspiring. As I began to focus more on the rainbow, the pot of gold meant less and less. I made enjoying the journey more important than worrying about the destination—not because I was enlightened, but because I had been aiming for the destination and hitting it, but not feeling good, so what was the point?

I never chased money, or success; I chased the feelings that accompanied those things—feelings of acceptance, significance, connection, and simply being seen. I was able to scratch a lot of those itches by being more creative and collaborating with dope people. Doing it this way is much less taxing than the logistical, administrative game of Jenga I was playing by booking my own shows.

I haven't performed in London since, and when I do again, it will be dripping in effort and fun. I won't think about getting through to the end of the show. Instead, I'm going to enjoy every moment of it, dancing on that rainbow, knowing that the journey is the only treasure that matters.

I MADE ENJOYING
THE JOURNEY
MORE IMPORTANT THAN
WORRYING ABOUT
THE DESTINATION.

11

GIVE YOURSELF PERMISSION TO DANCE ON DIFFERENT RAINBOWS

I have vivid memories of listening to an N.W.A cassette* as a kid and falling in love with hip hop. The music was laced with profanity and ideas I had never heard before, and the energy was magical. The diss tracks, extreme violence, hard-hitting beats, and rhythm connected with me instantly. I found myself rapping around the house—putting rhymes together, making up songs, just doing it for fun. Rappers didn't look like me, rappers didn't come from Canada, there wasn't an inch of me that thought rapping professionally was something that was possible.

Isn't that how most things go?—we create the reasons why amazing things can't happen to us.

I never stopped writing though. In high school, I was on online hip hop forums participating in battle raps and taking deep dives into lyric booklets, studying rhyme schemes and cadences. But I wasn't ready

---

* Yes, cassette. Google it, and N.W.A, if you have to.

to let others see that part of my identity yet because, again, I don't fit the bill for a rapper, so I would stand around when rap ciphers formed, too scared to share my voice, afraid of judgment, afraid of making a mistake, afraid of embarrassment, afraid of failing.

Instead, I kept writing behind the scenes. I started writing poems for my friends to give to their girlfriends, and they loved them. Sixteen-year-old me could whip up a rhyme very quickly, add a theme, sprinkle the right amount of corniness, and then send it off to a lovely lady, who would never know I wrote it.

At university, I went to a concert and saw a spoken-word artist by the name of Ian Kamau perform. There was no music, only rhyme, emotion, energy, and stories, and I was instantly hooked. I'll never forget when he said, "Like a fine wine, we'll get better with time," and the ladies in the crowd melted. I bought his CD, studied his work, and decided I could try spoken word—and, I hoped, win some girls over in the process.

Isn't that how most things go?—we take amazing risks only so we can impress others, and maybe get laid.

I began writing spoken-word pieces on my computer and printing them out and pasting them into this Edgar Allan Poe notebook I owned. I attended a poetry slam in a small coffee shop, and out of six participants, I came in second place.

Humble the Poet was born.

From there the pieces came together. It wasn't long before I began to write with music in the background, and my voice snapped onto the beat. Spoken word on a beat is a form of rapping, and I never looked back. I learned to record myself and release shitty quality freestyles on YouTube every day, and slowly I found an audience.

Fast forward a few more years and I was a full-blown recording artist, working in a nice studio, collaborating with producers who made dope music, and shooting videos with friends who were great behind the camera.

Then I went full time, and everything changed. I was a rapper.

Yet the upward trajectory was short-lived. I relied on freelancers, for whom my gigs were one of many. One day my video guy got in a fight with his girlfriend and stopped picking up the phone. My studio engineer invested in a new DJ company and became harder to reach. I suddenly had a computer full of music that needed recording but didn't know anyone else who cared enough to record it with me.

Isn't that how most things go?—we pile up our expectations on others to make stuff happen, and when they can't deliver, we're disappointed, lost, and confused.

At that point I didn't know what to do. I didn't have the technical skills to release music at the quality I needed to, and I didn't have the bank account or time to start learning. I was writing here and there but unable to record or share my work publicly, and ultimately I felt stifled waiting around for people to get back to me. I was stuck.

In the age of social media, the easiest way to retire, or quit, is to just stop. No need for an announcement; there's so much noise on people's feeds, very few will even realize you stopped contributing. I felt like I was becoming invisible because I had nothing to share.

I read about a guy who blogged every day, and the number one question in his FAQ was "How do you come up with things to write about?" And his response was, "Just keep writing, you'll be surprised how much you have."

I had never focused on writing anything nonmusical before. Whenever I read books by other people, I would fantasize about being an author, but, like with rap, I had a list of reasons why being an author was for other people with magical skills or awesome life stories, not me. I was too far out of my comfort zone.

But blogging—that sounded like something I could do. I had a folder on my computer titled "Hot Pix," which was not full of porn, but rather, super interesting images I had collected over the years. I had the idea to free write about each image and then post it out into the world.

But the self-doubt crept in.

People don't like reading long-ass captions; attention spans are fading.

People come to you for music, not to read your opinions.

You're going to push people away and confuse them.

You're not qualified to write about things.

People only want music videos.

You're a rapper, not a writer; writing is lame, rap gets the girls.

What if you run out of pictures?

People are going to think you quit music because you weren't doing well.

Isn't that how most things go?—you come up with a great idea, and immediately make a list of reasons not to do it.

Even though I had conquered self-doubt when it came to entering music, I found myself in the exact same place again. With music, I was obscure and unknown and could hide behind lyrics and videos. Now that a good chunk of people knew who I was, this new project felt even more difficult.

Isn't that how most things go . . . no, not this time. This time we're just going to keep moving and pull the trigger. That trigger was hitting POST.

And I did.

I wrote every day. I picked a picture out of the folder and wrote about it. At that point I had learned a bunch of lessons from all my missteps as I transformed from Teacher to Artist. I had no shortage of things to say.

Eventually, I ran out of pictures, but I kept writing. Within a month, the most popular comments on my posts were, "Wow, I needed this!" and "How are you living in my head?" I realized that telling my stories was helping other people figure out their own.

When I did music, it was so layered that the content wasn't absorbed as directly as my posts were. People responded to my writing when I just laid it out in black-and-white text.

People don't like reading long-ass captions; attention spans are fading.

Some people left, more new people showed up . . . and stayed.

People come to you for music, not to read your opinions.

Some people complained, more people encouraged me to keep going.

You're going to push people away and confuse them.

No one was confused—people deserve more credit than that.

You're not qualified to write about things.

When the things I write about have to do with me, I'm the most qualified.

People only want music videos.

People want stuff they can feel, whether it's a music video, picture, cupcake, or long-ass caption.

You're a rapper, not a writer; writing is lame, rap gets the girls.

Rap is the most evolved form of literary art to ever exist; writing in prose isn't as difficult, and my audience quickly turned into mostly females, who did not know my music but came to get a copy of their book signed. All my homeboys, who helped with the shows, really appreciated that.

What if you run out of pictures?

Ideas kept flowing.

People are going to think you quit music because you weren't doing well.

That happened—a very popular YouTuber said that to a mutual friend, and he defended me because he saw what I was doing.

After a few months, the top comments on my posts became "You should write a book."

See, I had built a cage around my reputation, something no one else held the key to, except me. We all do it. **We plant our flag of identity into some lifestyle, or belief, or brand, or political party. Then we dig in deeper if anyone challenges that identity, but what happens when the doubt and challenges come from within?**

The artistic itch I needed to scratch all along was putting words together. It didn't matter if they were in poems, prose, bars, or screamed out in the shower; the words just needed to be put together. Our chosen/destined purposes are never very specific. We don't need to be working in a refugee camp in Bangladesh to fulfill our purpose; we just need to find opportunities to help those who need it—wherever they are and however we can. I never needed to be a rapper; it was just a way to add some "cool" to my dweeby obsession with syllables. I had to give myself permission to let go of an identity that no longer fit.

We're all on journeys, and sometimes we spend so much time on and invest so much energy in heading in one direction that the idea of any other direction is both foreign and frightening. Our journeys themselves become comfort zones, and sometimes hopping off one rainbow and onto the next is exactly what we need. Other times we may realize that the path we were on helped reveal the path we should be on, and that adventure of twists and turns will last our lifetime, and that's okay. No one needs to have everything figured out, and honestly, nobody really does, even if their social media posts present a different picture.

I HAD TO
GIVE MYSELF
PERMISSION TO

LET GO OF AN

IDENTITY THAT

NO LONGER FIT.

I didn't abandon music—rather, the opposite. Entering the literary world helped with my music and vice versa. Your generous purchase of this book will help fund my next music project, and now the music exists independent of anyone else's financial support. That means I can enjoy making the music I like, enjoy shooting the videos I want, and have few expectations for how things play out once I share my creativity with the world.

I've also found other mediums to share the words I put together, including fashion, public speaking, and filmmaking. None of those pivots would have been possible had I not allowed myself to adjust my sails and explore where else the winds of life could take me.

Now that's how most things go for me—I allow myself to have many paths.

Conquering the fear and getting started is essential, but doing that once doesn't make it any easier to do it again. If it had, I would have discovered Humble the Author much earlier, but now, at the very least, I am actively searching for what else is hiding in this beard to better define my reasons to exist.

NO ONE NEEDS TO HAVE EVERYTHING FIGURED OUT, AND HONESTLY, NOBODY REALLY DOES.

12 WE ALL HAVE DIFFERENT RAINBOWS

I had the opportunity to meet Pharrell Williams on a shuttle bus to a multiday conference and invited myself to pick his brain. I peppered him with questions about his biggest hit, "Happy."

"How do you keep making music after creating something as epically massive as 'Happy,' I mean, do you try to re-create that energy again? Is it even possible? Are you afraid that your best days are behind you?"

He paused and asked me a question in return.

"Why are you asking me all this? What are you struggling with?"

He saw a pattern in my questions; he knew I wasn't asking as a fan or as someone who was speaking because he had a rare opportunity to speak to the one and only Pharrell Williams. I was asking as someone desperate and thirsty for guidance.

And he saw that.

More importantly, he saw me.

At that moment he saw me better than I ever had seen myself. I told him I wanted to fill the void that my favorite rapper, André 3000, left with his retirement, and he replied, "You need to fill the Humble the Poet void instead."

I was speechless.

He continued, "Listen man, the sun will shine on you differently."

My shoulders dropped at least an inch, and I let out a sigh of relief.

The sun will shine on you differently.

I was comparing myself to everyone and anyone I encountered. If I was making music and met a well-off stockbroker, my mind would ask, "Why aren't you selling stocks?" When money got better, but I met someone with a beautiful body, I'd ask, "Why aren't you spending more time in the gym?" I would identify all the gaps in my life on the basis of whomever I crossed paths with. That's a dangerous thing because everyone we meet will always have something we don't have.

I had past success, but I hadn't achieved a win lately, and the more people I spent my time around—especially in circles of high achievers—the more I felt like I wasn't good enough.

I had lost my perspective; I was competing with the success of my past and was frustrated because I couldn't re-create it. The only option seemed to be to travel a road that didn't excite me. I had reduced myself to freestyling over popular Taylor Swift and Katy Perry songs, to ride the trends of their releases. I was also trying to wiggle my celebrity friends into my work and use their names for additional exposure. It was a road of chasing trends and riding coattails. Although that road wasn't exciting, I was terrified that my best days were behind me, so I was open to anything. No one wants to get trapped in their glory days; we all want to know the best is still yet to come.

Pharrell was right. When our shuttle arrived at the conference, I thanked him and we went our separate ways for the evening. He gave me so much to think about—and even more to feel.

Lilly, who was sitting beside me the whole time, and had actually broken the ice to start the conversation with him, simply said, "Yo daag, mans saw straight into your soul."

Translation: Did that really just happen?

I didn't go near Pharrell over the next few days of festivities. I was overcome with everything that had already happened, I didn't have anything new to contribute, and I wasn't going to try to slip him some music or make some superficial request for career advice. I didn't want to ruin the moment. But I did want to express gratitude and gift him something someone special had gifted me, a bracelet, and share with him a piece she wrote about him, hoping it would make us square for the sack of epiphanies he smacked me with.

When I approached him, he gave me the nugget of wisdom that still sticks with me: "I want to tell you something: your purpose isn't to make music, it's to ask questions."

I was left speechless yet again. Yet I struggled with his advice.

But music is my heart, it saved my life, and I'm fucking dope at it. Isn't that my purpose?

I couldn't muster anything to say, or process whether I was being insulted or inspired.

After that, we parted ways, and I've never crossed paths with him again.

Nine months later, I was having a cup of tea with the amazing author André Alexis. When he said to me, "The artist's job is to keep the important questions alive," my shoulders dropped once again. I realized what Pharrell had been telling me: I need to ask more questions. That's my purpose. That's how I will contribute.

I'll never know Pharrell's exact intentions for saying what he did, but I can share what it felt like and whispered to my core.

Don't make music for the sake of making music—you're not here for that, leave that to other people. Don't worry about what works and what doesn't. Birds don't sing for any other purpose but to sing. You create to ask the important questions, to protect the questions from vanishing, to ask the essential questions on behalf of those who haven't yet found a voice to ask questions themselves. You ask questions to continue carving and discovering your authentic self.

I didn't have an opportunity to agree or disagree when Pharrell spoke, because my body made the decision the moment my shoulders dropped. I was already always asking questions, but I thought I needed to share the answers to those questions in my art. Pharrell helped me realize it was more important and purposeful to share those questions in my work instead. The questions never age or change. They can be reshaped and polished and repackaged depending on the audience, but their purpose remains the same—to dig deeper and explore.

We often compare ourselves to others and use that as a metric to determine whether we're on the right path. Do we have enough followers, are we making enough money, are we creating a big enough impact? "Enough" is an abstract idea that finds its place on a spectrum, depending on whose lives we're envying at the moment. **Figuring out our gaps in comparison to others is always going to be an endlessly miserable experience.**

I watch my friends accomplish great things, and I want the same for myself, but I've been sowing different seeds, so I'll be growing different fruit. The truth is, I was clutching at a moment, hoping to wrap myself in it for all eternity and live off it forever, but that's not how it works.

You—like me—have a role to play, and I'm not going to get into a debate on whether that role is predetermined or a choice you make; just have fun figuring it out. We can free ourselves of the pressures of having to always have something to show for our work, or the journey we're taking, by just doing what we do. **The water doesn't know how it contributes to the pearl, and it doesn't need to.** Maybe if it did know, it would do a shittier job of it.

Walk your journey and live your truth, and find smiles and relief knowing that you're part of a bigger puzzle and your contribution is as important and insignificant as everyone else's. Share your journey with others, as they'll help you better understand yourself.

The sun will shine on you differently.

YOU—

LIKE ME—

HAVE A ROLE TO PLAY.

OFTEN, THERE IS NO END TO THE RAINBOW

If you play football, you want to win a Super Bowl; if you play poker, you want to win the World Series of Poker; if you're a nerd like me, you want to do a TED Talk.

Doing a TED Talk felt like the pinnacle goal for my life. It would mean that a bunch of smart people decided I was smart enough to join them in a room and pay me exactly twenty minutes of their precious time to hear what I had to say. Not only is it extremely validating and a great way to stroke the ego, having a TED Talk on your résumé is a great way to get other high-paying speaking gigs. When I get too old to rap, I'll still be able to wheel around in my futuristic wheelchair and do talks.

I've been invited to speak at TEDx events around the world, which, in contrast to the official TED Talks given at the annual conference, are independently thrown by individuals and their communities. As flattering as the invites were, my ego would quietly but sternly whisper "Naw, daaag, we're doing the real one, and nothing less."

This is the point of the story where I should have had an epiphany about the dangers of seeking outside validation to find my self-worth, especially when that idea is drizzled in almost everything I write, but that didn't happen. Stroking one's ego is a form of masturbation without any satisfaction, and it becomes addictive. Besides, I had accomplished enough in my life to know that nothing was impossible. Doing a TED Talk wasn't a matter of IF, it was a matter of TIME. It felt like doing one TED Talk was all I would ever need to feel validated on this planet as a writer, speaker, and intellectual.

So I continued to put it out into the universe.* Once my first book started selling well, I figured this would help roll the red carpet into the TED community. In reality, no red carpet arrived, but I was still eager to do a talk. Then, a friend involved in the TED Talks said I would be a great addition to the TED Fellows program and connected me with the team through email.

The TED Fellows program takes creatives and plugs them into the TED community, providing them with unique experiences and training and ultimately an opportunity to do a talk on the TED stage once they're ready. To put it simply, it's a golden ticket into the community and a fast track to doing a TED Talk.

The TED team emailed me to let me know that the application process wouldn't begin for another eight months, but they would love to have me attend the TED conference in Vancouver. I was on the fence—I wanted the fast track to getting onstage instead of watching it from a chair in the auditorium—but I agreed.

Of course, I waited until the last minute to book my travel and accommodations, but I made it to Vancouver to attend the talks, and instantly I was a kid in a candy store. The convention center was equipped with amazing displays and large screens for anyone who

---

* By "putting it out into the universe," I mean that I just kept telling anyone who'd listen.

didn't want to sit in the main hall. They had desks and hammocks and caffeine and gadgets and gizmos; it was a nerd's paradise.

During lunch on the first day, I ran into Riz Ahmed, a fellow rapper and rising Hollywood star, and he invited me to participate in a lunchtime discussion surrounding #MeToo and #TimesUp. Through that discussion I made some new friends. After another break, I ran into more people I knew, and by the end of the day, I found myself at a restaurant with some amazing people having delicious Punjabi food.

I had initially been hesitant to attend the conference. Why spend so much money and time traveling when I can watch the talks online later? TED Talks were already my go-to procrastination method, it didn't seem to make sense to see someone talk live, it wasn't like there would be pyrotechnics or music—but I'm glad I took the leap.

The energy in the main hall during the talks was electric. It's the same reason we watch sports events live: to feel a part of something bigger than ourselves. Plus, seeing the star players didn't hurt. I saw Al Gore stand in line for a good seat, just like everyone else, and I got to shake Steven Spielberg's hand as I passed by him to grab my seat. I laughed, I cried, I took pages of notes, and every night we partied and had fun.

I met a new friend named Chris, who overheard I was from Toronto and let me know he was a Buffalo boy. Being border buddies, we regaled each other with obscure Canadian trivia. Turns out that Chris was Chris Sacca, owner of one of the most successful investment funds in history and was a Guest Shark on *Shark Tank*. He was an active member of the TED community, and when I told him about my intentions to apply to be a TED Fellow, he not only offered to be a reference, but he also volunteered his time to look over my application.

He invited me to a private dinner he was hosting with his friends on the final evening of the conference, and I got to meet some of the most interesting people from all walks of life. I met some of the biggest names in tech, activism, art, and finance. My goal here isn't to name-drop, but to share an interesting room of people I had the opportunity to meet because I took a chance and bought a plane ticket. By the end of the conference, I'd met people who would become close friends and had found inspiration for creative projects like the one in your hands.

Chris Sacca kept his word and helped me with my application. He even gave me three rounds of notes and edits to get it just right. That application got me a phone interview with the TED team, and I felt that went great; I spoke from my heart and connected with the team.

Nonetheless, a few months later I received an email from the TED team thanking me for my application and interview, but unfortunately, they were not able to offer me a position as a Fellow.

If I'd received that email right after I'd applied—and before I'd gone to the conference in person—I would have felt pretty shitty. I'd have needed to sit for a few minutes and feel bad before giving myself a pep talk to feel better. But that's not what happened. The entire experience of taking that leap of faith to attend the TED conference had shifted my priorities. In my past, I had hesitated dozens of times when presented with opportunities because I didn't know whether they would pay off in the end. I began to realize over time that the opportunities themselves were the payoff, regardless of whether they turned out the way I wanted them to.

The truth is, even if I had become a TED Fellow and eventually had done a TED Talk, there would have been a day after, in which the shine of my achievement would fade and I would be searching for something else to keep my feeble ego happy. Enjoying the journey of the entire conference reinforced my love for learning communities, and it ultimately changed my way of thinking. My goal now is to no longer simply do a TED Talk, but to find as many think tanks and learning communities as possible to keep my fire lit. I really was a kid in a candy store, and had I attended that event knowing I had to do a talk, I would have been much too stressed and nervous to enjoy any of it.

The friends I made along that journey are far more valuable than anything else I could have achieved. They're what made it fun, and it's the fun that really matters. There was no pot of gold at the end of that TED rainbow, and that's okay—those are the best type of rainbows. Jumping into anything with low expectations is the best way to exceed expectations, so keep that in mind when deciding your next move. I've been to award shows and had a blast, while my friends who were nominated were nervous wrecks; sometimes the end goal sucks out the fun, so let's not focus on that when we take the journey.

I may never do a TED Talk, and that's okay; I'm going to have as much fun on this journey as I can, and enjoying it is the real reward for taking a risk and putting myself out there. **When you're enjoying the rainbow, the pot of gold only gets in the way.**

JUMPING INTO ANYTHING
WITH LOW EXPECTATIONS
IS THE BEST WAY TO
EXCEED EXPECTATIONS,
SO KEEP THAT IN MIND
WHEN DECIDING
YOUR NEXT MOVE.

CLOSE

The last birthday gift I gave myself was a tattoo on my hand that reads "now." I was going through a challenging time, and all I wanted to do was feel like a kid again.

Remember going outside to play as a kid? Whether it was at recess or in the neighborhood, you ran, you jumped, you worked and burned calories, and you made decisions and laughed and cried and scraped you knees—and that was it. You didn't get a paycheck for doing it; the only reward was, well, doing it. You didn't need anything else, you were having fun. You lost all track of time when you were having the most fun.

As we grow up, what it means to play evolves. We have less time to do things, and there are so many more options that *look* fun that we keep trying them all. Not all of them make us feel as good as we did playing outside as kids, but then again, ain't nobody got time for that anymore. We just want something quick, easy, and convenient. The older we get, the more responsibility comes our way, and we have to get stuff done by a certain time, whether that's pay rent, submit an assignment, write a book, find a soul mate, or catch up on a new episode before the internet spoils it. More and more things begin to come with a hump just off in the horizon, and all we have to do is get over that hump, and we'll feel a little lighter.

Then we get over the hump, only to see new humps in the horizon. We can't make time to really play until after we get over the next hump, or dream of hitting those lottery numbers so we can finally be free of all the humps.

The uncomfortable truth is that the humps don't end, even if we win the lottery, shed twenty pounds, or get hired as a Nutella taste tester. Our lives, and all the things worth enjoying in them, don't come after the humps—they *are* the humps. The ups and downs, problems and solutions, challenges and triumphs are what pave this journey. They don't always make it look pretty, but no one ever promised they would.

Realizing that we're better off focusing on the road we're on instead of pinning our hopes beyond the horizon can't happen overnight. It's not a switch anyone can flip. It's going to be a lifelong tug-of-war, which is the exact opposite of quick, easy, and convenient.

So why do it?

Because all of those quick, easy, and convenient fixes we chase take a toll on our mental, physical, and spiritual health, which causes a cycle that's going to doom us to a life of chasing fixes. Being mindful and aware of the present—what we're doing and whether we're enjoying it—can help take us back to the times when we lost track of time. The nerds like to call it *flow state*.

It's true, having things to look forward to is nice, especially since none of us is going to ever achieve a state of mind that has us constantly present. We'll always be jumping back and forth between our past and the future—that's never going to change. **I'm simply encouraging you to focus more on the present.** That means focusing on laying the next brick, knowing the castle will be ready when the last brick is laid and not a moment sooner, and then remembering that as good as it feels to enjoy the triumph of building that castle, there

133

will be a day after, and we'll have to find another castle to build—and that's okay.

Reclaiming any of our time is better than nothing, and just as things gradually shift from our childhood to where we are now, things can just as gradually shift back. We may not be able to pick our noses in public anymore, but we can focus on enjoying where we're at a little more than worrying about where we need to be.

Exit

We're not lost, if I'm lost with you
Paths crossed, eyes locked, and I saw you
Everything between now and forever
When I'm with you, it's now, forever
I don't care where we're going if I'm going with you
So many hard rights and sharp lefts
We've done quite a dance
And I don't know when our song will end
Or if someone else cuts in
I'd rather own today than to borrow tomorrow
Finish line when we finish time
Not a second before or after

ZOOM OUT

Enter

You belong with the evil over there
You fed off my trust, and needed me to care
Needed me to share
Meeting you was the worst thing
Losing you was even worse
I'm a magnet for bad days and blood suckers
No gift, only curse
Why god makes someone like you
Why, god must be someone like you
Someone, despite who, has a ray of sun
Focuses it only on what they can burn
You'll never learn
I'll never learn
No one cares that I'm tired
No one is giving me a break
No one bothers to help or could ever understand
I'm drowning in a sea of the selfish
Even though you're not here, you're still my anchor
   Light doesn't shine this deep

OPEN

I was in Delhi helping at the grand opening of a new club called Shroom, which looked like a giant mushroom from the inside. I was Tetris-stacking gift bags from expensive brands, and when I met the owner I congratulated him on the success of his new club. His response surprised me.

"Oh, I don't care about this place anymore, it was only fun while we were building it, and now that it's done, I'm thinking about the next one."

He then had me stand up straight and extend my arms to the side. There I stood in the middle of this nightclub, looking like Da Vinci's Vitruvian Man, wondering what I was doing.

He explained: "Imagine the length of your wingspan representing all of existence; if that's the case, then human history represents only half the surface of the tip of your middle finger. None of this shit matters."

Then he walked away, leaving me standing there, arms wide out, wondering how I continued to meet these magical creatures.

The big picture is hard to see when we're a part of the artwork. It's very easy to fall into existential dread and develop a center-of-the-world mentality if we don't take a second to step back and see what else is going on. When we focus on only ourselves and the isolated incidents that happen to us, we become disconnected from everything and everyone else, and that has an isolating effect.

I would love to complain that gas prices are affecting only me, but those exact same prices are hurting people who earn far less and need more fuel. In order to recognize that, I need to get out of my head, and my own personal universe, and zoom out to get a better view of how things affect more than just me. This helps me to take things far less personally and to find opportunities for gratitude.

Zooming out helps us to think more in the long term and recognize patterns so we don't overreact in the short term. Life isn't what happens to us; it's how we deal with it, and how we deal with it always depends on the perspectives we can find. Zooming out helps us realize that the story is still playing out, and we shouldn't rush to any conclusions.

Taking out the detail and having a birds-eye view of a situation can also help us relate better to others and the challenges they may face. We may not be afraid of spiders, but we do know what it means to feel paralyzed by fear. We may not have stolen money, but we know the feelings of hopelessness and desperation and what we're willing to do when our backs are up against the wall.

Taking a step back helps us realize that we can't predict the future, so we shouldn't be so quick to judge the present. Many of us have been around long enough to see something that seemed like great news turn into the opposite, and vice versa.

Zooming out also helps us realize how insignificant things are in the grand scheme. Sometimes we get so caught up in the minor problems of life that they begin to feel major. Having a moment to pause and gain more insight will help us take off the blinders and get a better picture of who we are, where we are, and how we fit into the larger story. Acknowledging how small we are can be frightening, but also very liberating.

The goal of this section, and the book as a whole, is to help you spend less time judging life and more time understanding and embracing it. Pausing and zooming out is a great first step. It'll help you build compassion for others, which in turn strengthens the empathy and compassion you can show toward yourself. And the better you feel about yourself, the better the life you'll lead, so don't be afraid to zoom out some more.

14

TRY TO RELATE TO THE BAD GUYS IN YOUR STORY

For some people, there is absolutely nothing more wretched and amoral than infidelity. How dare someone exploit the loyalty and trust of someone else? It's inexcusable. I always saw cheating as something weak people do. People get in relationships with people who don't match, but because they don't have the nerve to end it, they go and do hurtful things in secret instead. Love should be enough to stick with one person for the remaining two-thirds of your life, and if you can't, you're a failure. Anyone who cheated and got caught was a lowlife, and anyone who was cheated on and forgave was desperate and pathetic.

But that thinking changed when I entered the holy trinity of cheating, meaning, that I've:

- Been cheated on
- Been the cheater
- Been the dude someone cheated with[*]

---

[*] Knowingly and unknowingly.

I was cheated on and I forgave—how pathetic of me, right? She called me and told me that during a party she had too much to drink and doesn't remember anything, but her friends said they saw her making out with another guy. I was initially shocked, but she came clean and wasn't trying to hide it, so how mad could I be? I thanked her for letting me know and got off the phone. Only after I'd hung up did I begin to feel my emotions bubbling up. I called back and let her know I was upset, and then she got upset because I wasn't allowing her to rid herself of her guilt.

"I don't even remember doing it, my friends weren't even sure it was me with the guy."

But don't your true feelings come out when you're drunk?

"I didn't even have to tell you, and as soon as I found out, I did."

But why did you feel the need to do it in the first place? Why are you annoyed with me for being hurt?

I got cheated on, and it wasn't pretty.

I also was the cheater, which I hate admitting.

I'm good with words, and it has always been fun to see how well I could sweet-talk someone—anyone. After another long-term relationship dissolved on me, I looked to drown myself in other women. I flirted with any and every girl who was warm to it—not because I wanted to sleep with all of them, but because their receptiveness made me feel good, it made me feel special, it made me feel seen.

I set parameters around myself and the girls in my life, too afraid of getting close because I was still injured from the past, but also in desperate need of anything that would take my mind off the pain. The irony, of course, was that I didn't remember **I'm not just a victim of pain: I'm capable, like all of us, of creating it in others.**

It was during this period of distracting myself with fleeting relationships that I became someone I'm not proud of. Someone who, when slapped with the three words "What are we?" would always give a fuckboy response like "We are what we are," knowing that the question deserved much more of an answer.

I became someone who finally went too far. Someone who didn't realize what that meant until I heard her voice, trying her best to be strong. I deserved to hear a resounding FUCK OFF; I didn't deserve to have the power to hurt her. I could hear the cracks in her voice, and the call ended before a tear dared touch her cheek.

And finally, I was the dude someone cheated with.

After I abandoned relationships for more of the playboy lifestyle, some of the women I came across were already seeing someone. Most of them didn't want me to know, but I'd eventually find out. They'd be vague when describing that there was another guy in the picture and would paint him as either someone who was just pursuing them or someone from the past. The truth was really that I was an exciting change. I was low maintenance, convenient, and shared their priority for discretion.

Every woman I dated who already had a boyfriend represented something to me, to make up for what I felt was an inadequate life before I got into the arts. I felt like I had to play catch up and make up for all the fun I hadn't had before. But I was trying to feel better about myself by pursuing women who were out of my league. I didn't realize that I was headed in only one direction, and it wasn't up. The first person to warn me was Tupac.

In an interview, he attributed his past playboy lifestyle to insecurity, and once he found himself and his foundation, he'd found his queen.

Insecure? I'm the man! You see these girls I get?

It wasn't until years later that I saw Rabbi Shmuley Boteach break it down: "Men have affairs for affirmation."

Even with these warnings from minds I respected, these truths felt inconvenient, and I avoided them. I had to step back from myself and look at my entire situation from a higher vantage point, without judgment, to realize the truth in their words.

All of these experiences gave me a 360 view of cheating. Initially, I'd entered all of those relationships assuming something about the other person. I used to think of guys who got cheated on as sad, somewhat deserving idiots. I used to think cheaters were all apathetic assholes—I knew exactly who to label as the good guy and the bad guy. And I used to perceive the women who used me to cheat as shady man-eaters, and any other girl who could have her pick of guys would be the same.

I opened my mind only when I was able to step back, gain a wider perspective, and realize that everyone, including the girls who did me wrong, were all simply people trying their best with the tools they had. This perspective was only truly cemented when I found myself in their shoes.

An apocryphal saying claims: "Everything in the world is about sex except sex. Sex is about power."

It's not good enough to just understand that we did something uninspiring, or that we've figured out the WHY behind it. The more we can step out of our situation, the more we can figure out what other behaviors and expectations contribute and relate to these same choices.

For me, part of the reason I went down the infidelity road is because I got caught up in the idea of the game. Being rich and successful is the unrealistic body type for all guys to measure up to: it's our bikini body. We read about the uber-successful, and all the stories focus heavily on the financial and professional achievements of such people, and that makes us feel like failures. In the face of that failure, we turn to the validation we get from women to feel like winners. Winning the game is an addiction,* but how we go about feeling like a winner has consequences.

If pictures of cancerous lungs can't get people off smoking, then what's getting caught cheating going to change?

From the outside in, cheating seemed like an easy thing for me to judge. From the inside looking out, everyone else seemed better. The perspectives I gained had me dead center, looking all around me, within me, and everything in between. Experience provided that perspective, but it was up to me to ensure I used these perspectives to make healthier decisions moving forward. Logic wasn't enough, neither was fear. I needed a punch in the feels.

I existed in this unholy trinity of infidelity, and maybe if I had experienced each of its parts in a different order, I'd have a different view of them. But the way I encountered them helped me recognize the common threads in all of them—once I was able to step back and organize my experiences.

They all involve fear, whether it's a fear of commitment, a fear of communicating our desires, or a fear of abandonment. These decisions are pushed by fear more than they are pulled by love, which will only lead to the very things we think we're avoiding. In many situations, the people we vilify for these choices are just scared and don't have the tools to address that fear. It feels better to see them as apathetic assholes—until we're one of those apathetic assholes ourselves. The only way to ensure we don't fall into the cycle is to have more compassion.

Looking back, I realize that my self-esteem doesn't just go up from getting that new girl; it also goes down from hurting the previous

---

* Who doesn't like to win?

one—making her feel invisible and insignificant. The irony is that I was blind to others but obsessed with being seen myself.

There aren't any bad guys, and the contempt and resentment we hold for those who do us wrong only pollutes us. We can forgive ourselves only when we're open to forgiving others. Forgiveness doesn't require an apology, nor is it saying, "I'm cool with what you did to me." Forgiveness is saying, "What happened sucked, and it hurt me, but I no longer want to carry it with me moving forward." Achieving a state of forgiveness takes more time for some people than others, and that's okay.

Our insecurities are the ultimate bully, and the less we cross paths, the better. We stay in line, adjust our lives, and hope never to be confronted by the bully. The world of love is still a fascinating and frustrating space for me, but I'm trying to move forward with as much self-awareness as possible. I check myself to see whether my insecurities are holding the steering wheel, and to recognize that I can be bold enough to have an open, honest discussion about this when someone is in my life.

These battle scars gift us insight, awareness, compassion, and resilience, and those who judge us for our choices are most likely doing so to avoid the issues they have with themselves.[*] Very little comes from prolonged self-pity and finger-pointing.

Cheating, much like crying over a breakup, is something we don't think we'll ever do until we do it, and then we quietly step off our high horse and fade into the shadows. Here I am instead, airing myself out, hoping to figure out how I got myself into those situations, so it doesn't happen again.

Maybe some of you reading this will find some peace in your

---

* We all love a good distraction.

decisions, and I hope that others will see their situation in a new light and save the calories it takes to judge and shame other people. We don't have to become the people we judge before we stop judging them. All we have to do is take a breath, pause, and zoom out from the situations we find ourselves in. Remembering all the times we said we would never, until we did—whether that was cheating in a relationship or breaking a diet or joining Amazon Prime. Having a complete view of infidelity not only helped me make healthier decisions about my personal relationships, but it helped me see patterns in other parts of my life where I chose short-term gratification over something more sustainable.

This section isn't for the holier than thou; it's for the people who want to look themselves in the mirror again, and the ones who don't want to lose someone who matters to them because they have chinks in their own armor.* Seeing a bigger picture, without judgment, is the only way we can have a clear view of the life and future we want, while being able to stomach inconvenient truths and without being left jaded, bitter, or blaming the world.

Forgive others, and forgive yourself—there's more than one way to see our flaws, and the flaws of those around us. Making a commitment to reserve judgment until we can take a step back can save us from more than just a heartache.

---

* Or should I say amour?

SEEING A BIGGER PICTURE,
WITHOUT JUDGMENT,
IS THE ONLY WAY WE
CAN HAVE A CLEAR
VIEW OF THE LIFE AND
FUTURE WE WANT.

15

CHAPTERS END, BUT OUR STORY AS A WHOLE KEEPS EVOLVING

I grew up in a Sikh household, but it wasn't always that way. A year into a job at the Kellogg's factory, my mother got injured and could no longer work. So she spent her free time at the gurdwara, learning about Sikh philosophy and history, and slowly that trickled its way into the house. My father quit drinking soon after, and we became the religious ones in the family. The family socialized less because my father didn't enjoy the heckles of his old drinking buddies, who didn't appreciate his change in lifestyle. We became vegetarian, and my mother took me and my sisters to the gurdwara to enroll us in Sikh-based youth camps whenever she could.

I'm a mama's boy, so I happily followed my mother's lead. At age seven I stopped cutting my hair. I went from a kid with a bowl cut to a kid with wild and untamed hair. I started tying my hair in a knot on top of my head and wrapping it in fabric in the third grade. Mom would share the most glorious stories of the heroes in the Sikh past. Sikh heritage is full of martyrdoms, all with the belief that sacrifice is worth it and God is always on your side.*

I thought about God sometimes, and I recited the chants and hymns like a parrot. Then when I was eight years old I began to talk to God directly. I had mistakenly cut the logo off my new Nike sweatpants while goofing off with some scissors. I sliced a hole right in the tiny Nike logo below the pocket. I shoved the pants in the back of my dresser that night, closed my eyes, and begged God to please fix the pants. I was full of anxiety, trying to figure out what I needed to do for God to save me.

Waheguru Waheguru Waheguru Waheguru, please fix my pants, waheguru waheguru waheguru . . .

The next time I checked, the hole was still there and my heart was broken. My first real prayer had gone unanswered.

A few days later, the pants were repaired, most likely by my mother, but I didn't get in trouble, and in some ways, I felt God had my back. God and I were still friends.

But by middle school, God was helping me less and getting in the way more. In the sixth grade, a girl passed me a note asking me whether I liked her. I did. She sat across from me, and for weeks we spoke every day. I knew she had a crush on me. The problem was, she believed in a different God than I did. So the day I got her note, because of my fear of God,** I replied to the note insensitively with a capital NO. I lost a friend and potential girlfriend that day. God and I were still friends, but we had some disagreements.

In high school, I was endlessly curious about God. When I walked my dog, I had open conversations with God. I talked about

---

* Even if your enemies believe the exact same thing.
** And my parents.

my problems, my dreams, my thoughts. My best friend at the time was heavy into the Bible and Rastafarianism, so we spent most of our time talking about our three loves: God, Dogs, and Girls. This is when I started looking at religions as different rivers all flowing into the same ocean. I didn't think it mattered if you were Hindu, Muslim, Christian, Sikh, Jewish, or Buddhist because we'd all end up in the same place at the end, and God loved us all equally. I also started being exposed to the idea of karma, that we reap what we sow, whether in this life, a past life, or the next. When a kid in my school died in a fire, I reasoned that it was God giving that kid payback for some dumb shit he had done in a previous life. We had to live righteously and trust that God would protect us. God and I were still friends, but it was complicated.

By university, I was beyond simple dogma and transitioned into the pragmatism of the philosophy that existed within Sikhi. No longer was I simply reciting hymns my mother had bribed me years before to memorize; I was dissecting their meaning and trying my best to apply them to challenges I was facing in life. I spoke to God every day, and when I bowed at the gurdwara, I would only say two words:

Thank you thank you thank you thank you thank you

In the years that followed university, God had my back, and I took responsibility to crack the codes of God's teachings. I looked for meaning and symbolism in everything, and when I suffered my first major heartbreak, songs about God brought me some solace. I wasn't concerned with the do's and don'ts of dogma anymore. I had transcended that. I was hanging out with the "I'm not religious, I'm spiritual" crowd, and the hip hop artists I obsessed over all believed and preached that they shared a God who considered them, despite the inequities and challenges they faced, to be special people on earth. God and I, at this point, were best friends.

Over the years, I met people who were atheists and I pitied them and their incessant need to feel alone in the universe. For me, magic was everywhere, and it was important to believe in something superior to myself—how else could I remain humble? Many of the atheists I met were hell-bent on being condescending and making theists feel stupid. At that point it didn't matter if they were right; I dismissed them because they were assholes.

Ideas of a world without God made me uncomfortable. Many times in my life, God was my only real friend. God was my internal light, and hearing smart people ask questions I couldn't answer wasn't the most pleasant experience.

But everything changed when I found a video online of a young man describing his journey from being pious to being atheist. He said a nonbeliever made a list of things that would persuade him God existed, which included things like

- Show me an undeniable miracle on command
- Show me a talking bush
- Raise the dead
- Change the time of day instantly

The list went on, but it wasn't the content of the list that was important. The important part was that the nonbeliever was open to the idea of believing if some sort of condition was met. Things got interesting when the nonbeliever turned the tables and challenged the theist to produce a list of things that would make him switch over to Team-No-God. The theist-turned-atheist who made the video admitted that when his friend posed this challenge, he felt there was nothing that could make him change his mind, and that realization started his journey. He believed in God, but he also wanted to be open-minded. Not providing someone with an opportunity or any conditions that could change your views is the opposite of being open-minded.

As an educator, someone committed to lifelong learning, and a person who found significance in being smart, I didn't want to be closed-minded. This man's question—what would persuade you that there is no God?—challenged me to find conditions upon which I would no longer believe. What I discovered left me silent. It felt like a breaking point. I didn't want to abandon my lifelong relationship with God, but I was no longer allowed the luxury of blind faith.

For instance, I'd always thought that people who don't believe in God also don't have morals because only God teaches moral lessons. But when I started talking to my atheist friends, I found more questions than answers.

> Me: "But it's important to believe
> that something is superior to us
> for us to remain humble!"

> My atheist friends: "How humble
> is it when you think you're so
> special that someone is always
> watching over you, and not the
> children who die every forty-
> five seconds from preventable
> diseases in Africa?"

I began to read more, question more, until my beliefs faded, slowly but surely; I could no longer believe, even if I wanted to. To be honest, I think something shattered inside me in that moment. For every chapter of my life, God had been there. God was a central character. Now,

God wasn't the best friend or even in the friend group. God now only played a small antagonistic role, at best.

It wasn't that God had become an enemy; it was more that God had become an idea, like a unicorn or a leprechaun or Santa Claus. I became aware of my own cognitive dissonance and confirmation bias. We see what we want to see, and believing in signs from the universe makes for a comforting cocktail.

Here's why this matters: My story continued. Of course, in the moments following the end of my faith in God, I couldn't see beyond the current chapter of my story. I had clung to that relationship. **Belief is a strong thing, and I can understand why so many people cling to it tightly, not wanting to give it an inch of air, fearing that it might fly away. Because once it does, it's not coming back.**

The death of my relationship with God came like any other death. My life flashed before me, I saw everything again, but with a new lens. Why is my hair long? Why is my head wrapped? Why are there so many churches and temples and mosques? If we're alone, why bother being a good person? Karma isn't real; there's no one in the sky watching me. Was I free, or abandoned?

Yet when I recognized that this was merely a chapter ending and that a whole bunch more was coming in my life, I started to see the big picture.

Our beliefs serve as pillars that hold up our identities. That's why it was so hard for me to let go of God, and why my grief when my faith ended was so powerful. But that isn't the end of my story. Since then, I've learned so much more about Sikh history, which helps me have a context for the philosophy without belief. I've studied scientific explanations for the cosmos and why we're here on this planet. Learning more about the universe and all its wonder keeps me in awe of and in love with creation, which in itself is a creator. It also reminds me of just how insignificant we are in the grand scheme of things, and that helps me build stronger connections with people. At the end of the day, that's all we're really searching for.

When I lost my relationship with God, I felt existential dread and the purposelessness of nihilism. What did life matter if no one was watching me and grading my report card? I've since moved on from that dread and have adopted an appreciation for all things big and small. It's a new chapter, one in which I'm liberated from the chains of the beliefs of others and am designing a life that feels more natural for me. I'm exploring my enthusiasms and obsessions. I envy anyone with enthusiasm and obsession, even if they are enthused about and obsessed with things that I'm not interested in. It's beautiful to see someone's eyes light up with love, no matter the object of their affection. There are plenty of people who don't believe in God but who still worship. The basics of their relationships and dependencies are the same, so who am I to judge? I can stay out of their way as I walk my own path.

I continue to question, and as I do so, my story evolves. With this new lens of seeing my faith journey as a piece of a larger puzzle, I've been able to see more of the landscape that piqued my curiosity. The shifts in my perspectives aren't tragic, they're normal, and who knows what the next thirty years have in store for this story—I'm open to it all. The more I zoom out and look at faith and belief beyond my own experiences, the more I realize how little I've been through, and there are so many more adventures to have and relationships to develop. I'm no longer tattooing a label (Theist, Atheist) on my forehead, because I've seen enough to know that this story, like every other story we have of our relationships, is still being written. I may come across a burning bush yet.

Faith is personal. This was my journey, and I share it not to try to influence you but to give you an example of something that will probably be an ever-evolving thing in each of our lives. Don't get frustrated if you haven't figured something out entirely yet, whether that be your job or your relationship or your faith. Some things are ever-becoming, ever-evolving. Stepping back to realize this is what matters.

Through my own process of stepping back, I embraced the reality that my current spiritual lens may change, but I'm not threatened by that. Time brought me here—to a place of self-awareness and patience. I still feel magic and beauty and inspiration. I still respect that people hold their own personal truths, and I win nothing by debating and trying to be right all the time. I'm not an atheist, agnostic, or theist. I am a part of life, and as science dictates, my matter cannot be created or destroyed, only redistributed.

So, while I'm here in my current form, I share gratitude and appreciation for everyone and no one for allowing me not to be stuck in nihilistic dread, or spiritual ignorance, and for reminding me that I'm going to be figuring this out until my final breath.

I thank my old friend *God* and my new friend *Time* for that.

TIME BROUGHT ME HERE— TO A PLACE OF SELF-AWARENESS AND PATIENCE.

16

JUDGE LESS, UNDERSTAND MORE

When I was sixteen I was homophobic. I didn't realize it at the time, because I didn't know any gay people and I lived in a universe where the words *faggot* and *gay* were generally used in the place of *lame*. No gay people lived in my neighborhood, and when I say "no gay people," I mean it wasn't a safe place to be gay, so no one ever admitted to being gay if they were. The irony is that I wore a turban and expected and fought to be respected for my choice at the same time that I was not respecting the lifestyles of others. As diverse as Toronto was, people still had to exist in pockets of the city that were safe for them. Where I grew up wasn't safe for homosexuals.

I was semireligious and decided that since sex between a man and a woman could create a child, being in a homosexual relationship was simply the pursuit of lust, and to sixteen-year-old hormonally confused and repressed me, lust was wrong.

I took "family studies" in night school during my last year of high school. It was seen as bird course—an easy way to bring up my grade-point average so I could get into university. I didn't even know what the course would consist of. The last time I had done anything related to family studies was in the eighth grade, and that was cooking meals and sewing pillows.

I don't remember the name of my teacher, but I do remember two things she shared on the first day. She had two daughters: One was a former stripper and the other was a lesbian. That was enough to make the class giggle. The course exposed us to worlds, thoughts, and ideas that we never would have been exposed to in the areas where we lived, and at sixteen that was exciting.

One day the teacher brought a guest speaker to the class and didn't explain who he was or what he wanted to talk about. The speaker split the class up between girls and guys and did a mind-mapping activity, asking all the girls to shout out answers to his question and writing down the answers on the board.

His question: How would you describe the ideal person you want to fall in love with?

That made the girls giggle some more, but they began to warm up to the exercise.

He has to be handsome!
Smart!
Sweet!
Good looking!
Rich!
Have a job!
Be nice to his mother!
Caring!
Stylish!
A good listener!
Strong!
Can fix things!

The list was funny, superficial, endearing, and some of the boys who had crushes on the girls in class took note. Whenever they said something unrealistic, like *rich*, all the guys groaned.

Once the girls' list was complete, he turned to the guys and asked the same question.

She has to be hot!

Know how to cook!

Great kisser!

Sweet!

Nice!

Polite!

Dresses well!

Loyal!

Caring!

Supportive!

Smells nice!

The board was filled with our ideal partner traits. Many of us (or at least me) had never dated anyone yet, so we were projecting our fantasies and what we saw on TV.*

We chatted about all the things on the board, and then the guest speaker asked a simple question: "Is there anything on the girls' list that can't be on the guys' list, or vice versa?"

We looked at the board intently, smart enough not to make sexist comments like *Cooking!* but also curious enough to realize that the qualities of an ideal girlfriend or boyfriend are pretty much the same.

He continued.

"I'm gay . . ."

To which some people in the class gasped and giggled, but he took it lightly.

". . . and I have realized that regardless of whether we are homo-

---

* Topanga and Kelly Kapowski always came to mind.

sexual or heterosexual, we all want the same things in the people we fall in love with."

I felt that in my heart. All the judgment I had placed on a specific group of people, even when I was a minority myself, was so unnecessary and ugly on my part, and all it took was a sincere and candid conversation for me to realize that.

He opened up the room to questions, and our teenage curiosities got the best of us.

Have you ever been with a girl?

When did you decide to be gay?

How did you know?

Are you afraid of God?

Do you have AIDS?

Most of us came from families of immigrants and religious households where the idea of being gay just wasn't an option. This was the first time we were exposed in a safe environment to someone who was gay where we could freely ask that person questions.

He answered every question as openly and honestly as he could. He was very nice about answering even the most insensitive questions, and I didn't realize then how important that interaction was. Before that day, gay people had been the *Other*, and this experience humanized them for a roomful of teenagers who barely understood themselves. That's how I'd found myself to be a homophobic sixteen-year-old who felt high and mighty talking about procreation over lust.* I took a step back, completely out of my universe, and saw not only a more accurate picture of the world, but who I'd become as a result of my closed-off ignorance. I was judging without information or understanding, and it didn't feel good to be that closed-minded.

---

* Something that was especially rich given that I'd never even dated anyone.

I didn't understand what it meant to be homosexual. All I knew was what I was raised to know. This closed me off to so much education and information, because I was afraid of something I didn't understand.

We judge people because it's easier than what we should be doing: trying to understand them. When we understand, we're less reactive and more compassionate. Trying to understand someone or something requires much more effort than judging, but it's so much more enriching in the long run.

The experience with the guest speaker at my high school family studies class didn't immediately motivate me to stop using intolerant language like "gay" instead of "lame," but it started the process of my shedding my homophobic biases. As I grew up, I was exposed to more people who lived, believed, and loved differently from me, and that served to expand my spectrum of understanding and compassion, because I no longer saw other people through a lens of fear.

There's a reason they call it divide and conquer, because once fear drives a wedge between ourselves and others, everyone is easier to control by those in power. Since I'd grown up without knowing anyone who was gay, I felt separate from all gay people, and eventually the homophobia that started in childhood took hold. Because I was a visible minority, other minorities were my allies, not my enemies. **Our common stories of oppression should unite us much more than our fears of each other can ever separate us.** My high school classmates and I feared something because we were told to. Fears download themselves through generations, not always in explicit ways. Our parents may not always be directly telling us who we can and can't love, or who we can and can't accept in our lives. More often, such messages are unspoken, and never updated.

It took a bold teacher with insights and resolve to shift the way a classroom full of knucklehead sixteen-year-olds thought.

This moment showed me the importance of being in uncomfortable situations and the growth that can result from them. It's easy to prejudge and avoid anything that isn't familiar, such as people whose life choices are different from ours, but that type of avoidance only causes isolation and closed-mindedness. I may not encounter a teacher who'll do the same for me again, but that doesn't stop me from being that teacher myself. I can continue to put myself in environments that require me to listen more and speak less, because that's where the learning, and growth, happens.

The more I understood, the less I feared, and the less I feared, the less I needed to control things by passing judgment on others. These emotions are universal to all of us, and we're light-years better off when we can be aware of when our fears are holding the megaphone. Think of all those people you've heard gossip about but have never met—whether they are public figures or just people you went to school with or work around. How many conclusions have you drawn about them? The ideas planted in our heads can paint unfair biases that can affect how we treat other people, and we need to catch ourselves when we do this and others when they try to do this to us.

I hesitate to say *Love is the way* because it feels clichéd and a bit too kumbaya, but letting another emotion besides fear hold the steering wheel can create some beautiful outcomes. We learn so much about ourselves and the world around us when we learn about other people. After the experience with the family studies special guest, I began to explore more people whom I had never truly understood. Some were inspiring figures who turned out to have fallen from grace, and others were individuals whose thoughts, actions, ideas, and words changed the trajectory of my life. All it took from me was a conscious decision to pause my judgments and step back to gain a wider view so I could better understand and learn from what I experienced. That commitment to having a broader perspective has enriched my life with new experiences, friends, and lessons I will hold close to my heart forever.

Live the way you wanna
Love the way you wanna
Play the way you wanna
Pray the way you wanna

TRYING TO UNDERSTAND
SOMEONE OR SOMETHING
REQUIRES MUCH MORE
EFFORT THAN JUDGING,
BUT IT'S SO MUCH MORE
ENRICHING IN THE LONG RUN.

17 YOU AREN'T THAT SPECIAL, EMBRACE IT

I had the honor of performing a poem for the Canadian Walk of Fame inductee ceremony, and I found myself at the studio nervously rehearsing a poem I had written only a day before. I waited until the last moment to get this poem prepared,* and now I had to perform it for national television and a roomful of Canada's most celebrated people. Right after I perform the poem, Dr. Roberta Bondar, the first Canadian woman to go into space, would give a presentation.

I stood backstage nervously as they mic'd me up. This wasn't live television, so if I messed up, they could yell "cut" and we could reshoot. But so far that evening, that hadn't happened, and the thought of being the only person who needed to stop everything and start over was terrifying.

I'm a classic overthinker, looking at everything from every angle, using my imagination as a weapon to beat myself up with the "what-ifs" of the world.

I overthink every conversation I'm about to have even before I have it.

I overthink weather, I can't leave the house without a sweater.

---

* This is a common theme in my life.

I overthink the things I say to people, and how they might react.

I overthink committing to people's invites.

I overthink my replies to texts/emails.

I'm overthinking writing this story.

Overthinking tends to be thinking about the worst-case scenarios, and it leads to a lot of decision paralysis. This situation was a classic case: I couldn't decide what to write for this important ceremony and found myself obsessing over it the day before. Now, unprepared and anxious, I was overthinking all the horrible things that could happen once I hit the stage to perform in front of all those people.

This was what I was thinking as a sound guy was trying to hide a microphone under my dress shirt, while trying not to touch me inappropriately.

Dr. Bondar was getting prepped as well, and I took that as an opportunity to quell my nerves with some small talk. I had always fantasized that I'd make it to the moon in my seventies and look down at Earth, the place where everyone I had ever known, loved, and hated lived. I'd put my thumb in front of my view and completely cover home, and then, in some super corny Casablanca fashion, I'd give Earth one last nod,* and then take off my space helmet, dying instantly and floating away into infinity.

I wanted to share that fantasy with Dr. Bondar, but I didn't, out of fear of weirding her out. So instead, I asked her a question: "Dr. Bondar, how did it feel to be in the space shuttle, seeing the entire planet from a perspective that only a few people have ever seen? Did that affect the way you see life?"

I hoped to hear a super inspiring response from her—as not too many people get to hang out in heaven and come back to talk about

---
* Or middle finger.

it. She had lived my dream of seeing Earth in all its glory—how could anything be exciting after that?

She smiled. "Well, it was a really nice view. I was able to see a lot of Earth from where we were, but never the whole thing. I think it's going to be much more transformative when we start traveling to Mars."

"Why's that?" I asked, semi-disappointed in her response.

"Because at one point, when traveling from Earth to another planet, we'll look out the window and won't be able to see either. It will be empty, cold, and lonely and will remind us of how insignificant we really are."

Even the stage manager who was setting up my mic paused after that. Everyone within earshot went silent, as they thought about empty space between our home and our destination.

Is that what Columbus felt when he was in the middle of the ocean?*

The more I thought about it, the more complex and frightening the thought became, and with that, a sense of peace came over me.

We are all so insignificant in the grand scheme of things, and even the grand scheme we understand is insignificant compared with the grand scheme we don't yet know, so stop worrying so much.

My performance went well, and Dr. Bondar, being the badass she was, gave an amazing speech afterward.

We get so nitpicky in our lives that we create stress and problems that don't really exist. We think the solution is to find a solution, but in fact, the solution is to step back, zoom out, and question whether all the pressure we're bringing down upon ourselves is warranted. When we do that, very rarely is the answer going to be "yes, it's war-

---

* But at least he could see water, right?

ranted," even in matters of life and death. What will that decision matter in centuries to come when we'll all be dead anyway?

That moment helped me when I was feeling a lot of pressure in my life, and it has become a litmus test for future pressures when I'm feeling overwhelmed.

In the grand scheme, this means nothing, because all of us are nothing, so have fun, and breathe in, breathe out, with a smile.

Lots of cultures and beliefs are built on the idea that humans are extra special, that creation exists for us, so they have pressured us not to squander our gifts. Those ideas may have worked when we had to look up at the stars for guidance, but eventually, we looked up long enough and came to a better understanding. Then we were able to go up there and start looking down at ourselves.

We chase significance and being seen, but there is so much more freedom in obscurity and insignificance, and when life gets its heaviest, that's the totem we need to bring us back.

WE THINK THE SOLUTION IS
TO FIND A SOLUTION, BUT
IN FACT, THE SOLUTION IS
TO STEP BACK, ZOOM OUT,
AND QUESTION WHETHER
ALL THE PRESSURE WE'RE
BRINGING DOWN UPON
OURSELVES IS WARRANTED.

18 WE DON'T OWN A CRYSTAL BALL, SO STOP ASSUMING THE FUTURE

I had two uncles who passed away far too early in life. Both men, who were brothers to my mother, had similar factors surrounding their deaths but completely opposite journeys to get there. One had some very good luck, and the other, enormous loss and suffering.

My mother grew up with one sister and four brothers; her older brothers are credited with sponsoring her move to Canada, which in turn brought my father and his extended family here as well. If it weren't for my older uncles, my mother wouldn't have married my father, and I wouldn't have been manifested in this handsome bearded form.

Before I was born, one of her older brothers won $100,000 in the lottery, which stretched pretty far in the 1970s, so he decided to move back to India to stretch those winnings even further. With a juicy bank account, and generational land, he didn't have to work—and developed a dependent relationship with alcohol.

Within a few years he died of alcohol-related complications, leaving behind a wife and three boys, the youngest a newborn. After he died it took another five years to bring his wife and children back to Canada where they lived in a modest apartment in one of the more challenging neighborhoods of Toronto.

My mother's other brother found his relationship with alcohol not after winning the lottery, but after his marriage turned sour. Following a bitter divorce, he quit his job and isolated himself from the family. Over the years, as I was growing up, we'd receive drunken calls from him reminiscing on happier times. He was a guest star at family functions, but I never knew him sober. His skin became so pale that, at my sister's wedding, a friend asked me who the white guy was who was crashing the festivities.

He was the brother who took care of my mother when she first came to Canada. Three weeks after she entered the country, they were involved in a car crash on the highway that claimed the life of the other driver. My uncle handled all the expenses and took care of my mom as her broken leg healed. She felt forever indebted to him, and even at his worst later in life, she tried her best to nurse him back to health, as he had done for her.

When he was married, my uncle and his wife had lost their first and second children at birth. This grief intensified when my uncle got divorced, especially since he was estranged from his surviving two children by that time. Even as his alcoholism worsened and dementia kicked in, his adult children had no interest in seeing him.

My mother, on the other hand, visited him every day at the hospital. He would speak to her as if it were thirty years ago in the village in India, with no concept of the present. My mother had him moved to a nursing home by our house, and a year later he died. One of his sons made it to the parking lot of the funeral home, but no farther.

One brother wins the lottery and drinks himself to death; the other loses two children, and then the rest of his family, and drinks himself to death. No one ever would have thought they'd have the same fate, given where they started.

When my second uncle died, I thought I understood the lesson: We can't predict the future. But there was more to it. It's true, we don't have control over many things, but we still can change some things—in particular, our awareness. In this case, it was the awareness of a common thread of substance abuse in our bloodline that had a tinge of cruel irony.

Years later, after I had performed at the Southbank Centre in London, my mother's eldest brother took me out to dinner. I asked him to tell me about his father, my grandfather. "Ah, my father worked hard," he said, "and provided for me to get set up to start earning so I could support the family from here in London. Once I did, he stopped working, and passed away within a few years."

"And how did he die?"

He looked off into the distance, "Oh, he drank."

Up until that point, I hadn't updated my James Bond vision of my grandfather (Nana Ji). I had heard he was in the military so assumed he had gone out to save the world and never came home. Unfortunately, this thread of alcoholism in my mother's family is nothing unique in the Punjabi community. Someone once told me to invest in a bar because "people drink when they're happy, and they drink when they're sad, so you'll always have customers."

Would things have been different if my uncle hadn't won the lottery? How many people ever think of the lottery as bad luck? Would things have been different if my other uncle hadn't lost two children or gotten divorced? We all have stories about something we think is bad news and then turns out to be not so bad. And we all definitely have stories about things we think are good news and then don't turn out that way. We can't see the future, and that simple fact is why we can't get too excited or worried about a situation; we just have to let it play out. Both my uncles reacted to their circumstances with either an optimism or a pessimism that were both unhealthy in hindsight. I can't hold that against them; they were young men in a foreign country doing their best with what they knew. Life is difficult for all of us.

And though we can't tell the future, we can pick up patterns. We can start to discover common threads in history to help us improve our present and future. Learning about my grandfather helped me see the pattern of alcoholism in the family, and that saved me from making some of those same mistakes. When we lose those near to us, we have an opportunity to honor their memories. **That honor can exist not only in our words, but in our actions.**

Learning from the challenges that those before me faced helps me avoid some of my own pitfalls. It reminds me not to get too excited or stressed about the future, and to learn about and adapt according to the patterns of the past. Those patterns are all we have, because we don't own a crystal ball.

Sometimes, deciding our futures is the reason they turn out the way they do. If we think something is bad news, we can make it worse. On the flip side, thinking something is good news can also serve to hurt us, because it may leave us with our guards down and encourage us to make decisions with more emotion than logic. The truth is, we don't know what will be good news or bad news in the end, and I keep the stories of my uncles close to remind me of that, whether shit is hitting the fan or the good news keeps pouring in.

There is no happy ending to this story—well, at least up to this point—and that's okay. It's a reminder to me that we can't see the future, so we shouldn't judge the present too quickly. Some people in my family have found themselves trapped in the same cycle of addiction; their choices and behaviors echo those of my uncles. Others have put my uncles' stories at the front of their minds and chosen more sustainable ways to cope with the challenges of life. They see the patterns in themselves, the family, and our Punjabi community as a whole, especially when it comes to substance abuse.

Mark Twain said, "History doesn't repeat itself, but it often rhymes," and we're better off trying to hear those rhymes and see those patterns instead of jumping to a conclusion that something is good news or bad. Often, "let's wait and see" is the better reaction.

I can't bring my uncles back, and I've had to make peace with the fact that I'll never know my mother's father, but the stories of their lives has gifted me insights that have been transformative. I make the effort to evaluate less and pay attention more, and I leave my faux crystal ball alone. Not knowing what's going to happen next doesn't frighten me; rather, it excites me. I've learned from my family's stories and have developed my resilience, so now I can handle whatever comes my way with open eyes, open ears, an open heart, and an open mind. **No matter how the events of our lives appear to be at first, let's take a step back, reserve judgment, and carefully pay attention as things play out.** Making this simple shift in perspective will help us find opportunities to improve how we feel about things along the way.

THOUGH WE CAN'T TELL
THE FUTURE,
WE CAN PICK UP PATTERNS.

19

ARE YOU BEING PUSHED BY FEAR, OR PULLED BY LOVE?

I write every day. Put on a beat, and the words fly out of me.

A full year into my journey of being a rapper and recording artist, I still didn't have any songs that had gained traction. Then one day, the masterful producer I work with, Sikh Knowledge, flipped an Algerian rhythm and posted it on his SoundCloud. When I heard it, I asked whether I could have it, and he didn't just take it off his page—he renamed it "For Humble" and saved it just for me.

A few weeks later, I wrote a song alongside my artist friends Hoodini and Baagi in their NYU dorm room. Everyone was sharing ideas, and something beautiful began unfolding from our collaboration. Baagi surprised the group in the middle of one of our writing sessions with a fresh box of Dunkin' Donuts. We celebrated this triumph, and I declared I was going to name a song after him and use the beat Sikh Knowledge had gifted me weeks before.

Go Baagi Baagi

We recorded the song, shot a really cool video, and put "Baagi Music" out.

Wow.

The song did more in a day than anything I'd released in a year. More views, more likes, more followers. I got so much attention, which was strange, but I loved it. Comments started pouring in—flattering, critical, and everything in between. People who had lost touch with me somehow found me. Women who had stopped replying to my messages suddenly wanted to catch up. Then I started getting emails offering me money to perform.

But there was another side to my sudden success.

A voice in my head, a quiet voice. Not the excited one that was soaking in all the attention like a little boy. There was a calm quiet adult voice in my head, and it said, "Don't fuck this up."

That voice would also ask questions like: "What if this is the last good thing you do?" "What if the people who helped you do this don't help you again?" "What if you're just a one-hit wonder?"

That voice found friends in the outside world. A very sweet and well-meaning friend in the music industry said to me, "You need to make another Baagi soon," which put pressure on me to re-create an organic moment that had happened with friends. My DJ, who also recorded, mixed, and mastered the song for me, said, "I still won't play this at parties, it's not that good." More self-doubt began to creep in.

Another friend, who I thought of as a little brother, heard the song and said, "Wow, you used to make real music and didn't care about popularity—now you just sold out."

He decided I wasn't a good influence on him anymore and he faded away from my life. The voice in my head sounded louder: "Look what success is costing you—is this worth it?"

Being a popular artist was something I had wanted, but having a song that was more popular than me wasn't.

When I started doing the shows, the audience would sit through

179

my opening songs, bored, until it was time for Baagi. I didn't know how to reconcile all of this, so I started pushing back.

I only made that song to prove I could; now it's back to my real music.

But no new music came

Because there was no fun

No excitement

No collaborations

No confidence

It was all fear

I overthought every word, every decision, every release, and crumbled under the pressure of having one successful song. The voices in my head found allies in the world around me, and together they beat me into paralysis.

We all have those voices, both around and, even stronger, within us. If we listen closely, we realize that those voices in our heads sound a lot like people we know. "You need to make another Baagi soon, or they'll forget about you." "You're only as hot as your last hit."

There are always moments when people say things that sting a bit harder than we expect. Their words set a new tone in our lives, a tone that makes us feel like we have to tiptoe around others and explain all our decisions, even if to an invisible audience.

We come up with ideas, and five seconds later we have a list of criticisms and reasons why they're bad ideas.

Maybe we want to wear our hair differently, but the voice tells us that people will think we're trying too hard.

Maybe we want to share a certain picture online, but the voice tells us that the only thing people will see are your asymmetrical eyebrows.

Since we were kids, we've been sponging up these voices, and slowly they've sucked the fun out of life and replaced it with fear.

We could still pretend that a cardboard box is a spaceship or have tea parties with our dolls, but we won't because those voices have told us so many times to grow up. Now nothing's fun, everything is a task, an errand, an item on a to-do list, or a straight-up job. Everything feels like work, even the stuff we loved, and in the end, we're scared to mess up.

After Baagi, I wasn't making music because I had something exciting to share; I was trying to keep my newfound career afloat. I was still working to grow my career, so I didn't see anything wrong with what I was doing. I thought I was leveling up, becoming more professional, more structured, and less raw.

But I was also afraid of never creating something as good as Baagi.

Then my friend Ryan Blair, a former gang member turned successful entrepreneur and author, told me: **"We're either pushed by fear or pulled by love."** Either way, he explained, we're headed in the same direction, but only love will keep us fueled for the long haul. Fear is not a sustainable motivator; it just exhausts us.

That voice in me, my inner critic, found power and authority when I entered an unfamiliar and uncomfortable space. When I was lost and confused, I turned to it because it sounded like all the people I knew growing up. I don't think I cared whether my inner critic was right—it just felt safe because that voice was so familiar. But in the end, my inner critic was exhausting me and my creative energy.

When we're scared and uncomfortable, we're drawn to the familiar, like a moth to light—often with the same consequences.

When Ryan said that to me, I realized that I was running off the wrong fuel. I would be lying if I said everything switched overnight. That's not how it happens in real life. Instead, I became more aware of this fear/love duality, and began checking myself, trying to restore the fun and excitement in my work, and my life.

I did this by going back to what else was familiar, but also healthy. That meant doing work purely out of love and excitement—no audience, no money, no expectations or entitlement. The only reward was the work.

I would love to tell you that now nothing feels like work and I'm dancing through life and earning a wonderful living in the process, but that wasn't the shift. The shift I experienced was the reminder to ask myself regularly: *Are you pushed by fear, or pulled by love?*

We need to ask ourselves what parts of our lives feel more like chores, like obligations, like work more than anything else, and how that feeling got there. A loving relationship between two people can get very complicated and heavy once they get married. Something that was seen as an end goal can open all sorts of new problems, and that's okay, as long as we're paying attention.

We have to take a few* steps back to see the whole picture, and not let our expectations of what we think things are supposed to feel like dictate our reactions. Because even the greatest things don't live up to the expectations we set for them.

I didn't know there was going to be a challenging side to having a hit song, but it prepared me for when the next hit arrived. New challenges will come from graduating school, getting a new job, losing our virginity, and any other milestones we daydream about. But we can be prepared, keep the fun alive, give voice to our inner critic, and then calmly brush that voice aside.

Chase the love, zoom out if you can't find it anymore, and take your time.

---

* Dozen.

FEAR IS NOT A SUSTAINABLE MOTIVATOR; IT JUST EXHAUSTS US.

CLOSE

When I was in teachers' college, I picked up a very inconvenient piece of information that was both frustrating and liberating for dealing with children. Our professor explained that children develop empathy over time, and so it's helpful to understand that they have a center-of-the-universe complex when you deal with them. They won't be able to instantly connect with others or think about how their decisions affect other people. They think about themselves, and slowly, through socialization mixed with the continual development of their brains, they can grow up to be compassionate and empathetic human beings.

Very little of this is useful when you're dealing with a child who just ate a tray of cupcakes meant for the whole class. They saw, their eyes got wide, and they ate. Asking them why they did it* won't yield any positive results. Often, you have to encourage the kid to go back into their limited memory and remember a time when someone took something that belonged to them, and ask how that made them feel and then hope they can connect that feeling to how they just made the rest of their classmates feel.

We're all that kid with a mouthful of icing and a dumbfounded look on our faces, struggling to see life beyond ourselves. We all

---

* As so many adults mistakenly do.

need to be aware of how our choices affect the world around us and how the world around us affects the choices we make. There aren't any more authority figures in our lives who will take the time to talk it out with us. Instead, if we cross any real lines, we'll end up in handcuffs and be reminded that ignorance of the law is not a good defense.

It is so easy to fall back into our younger ways and become self-absorbed. Our narcissism may not manifest as greed or being inconsiderate, but we may become hyperfocused on ourselves, unable to see anything beyond that. Politicians understand this, and that's why they appeal to our self-interests more than to our ethics and morals.

The challenge with thinking only of ourselves is that it further isolates us and makes it easier for us to take things personally. In the grand scheme, we are very insignificant, and as a population, we are very predictable. Often, those who hurt us are rarely plotting to do so but are just thinking of themselves too.

If we take a step back and accept these inconvenient truths, we can get more perspective on many of the bad days, events, and moments in our lives. This realization isn't a shortcoming that we need to address; it's just something we develop during our personal evolution. As adults, we don't need to empathize just with those people we harm; we also need to empathize with those who harm us. That means **we have to suspend judgment and focus more on understanding as much as we can.** That's challenging when emotions are involved, but it's not impossible. We don't have the tools to predict the future, but we can step back and notice patterns. That requires some clear vision—and recognizing when fear is fogging up the windshield on our journey.

When it's all said and done, more will be said than done, and we'll all return to the vast nothingness from which we emerged. That can be scary to think about, but also truly freeing, because it releases a lot of self-imposed pressure, allowing us to move toward the life we want.

Our inner children are still self-absorbed and struggling to connect and empathize with others, but **we have the power to encourage ourselves, with love, to see beyond ourselves, so that we can truly feel less alone and see the bigger picture of life.**

The view is so much nicer from up here.

Exit

Nani's wrinkles shared a path to paradise
I traced them with my fingers
She kissed my nose, and sang toothless poetry
Fluent enough to translate love
Less important than a grain of sand I am
Floating freely as if nobody needs me
Diving aimlessly into purpose
Focused on no where, to see all around
We don't have a life, we are a part of it
A river with currents of love, mapped on my Nani's smile

ZOOM IN

Enter

If anyone tried to pull the sad from me, they'd get tied up and roped in
It's a messy web, and once you're stuck, you're hopeless
I want to say more, but being quiet seems the best bet
Most would be happy to see my tears are melancholic
Made so many mistakes it's no wonder why misery finds me
The wise said I'll feel better in due time, but due time is hiding
I don't remember when things were ever good, guess I'm unlucky
It's sucky, knowing that life goes out of its way to fuck me

OPEN

I used to be super idealistic and rigid in my ways of thinking until life spanked it all out of me. I thought the good guys always won, and the bad guys would eventually fall, and I believed it was super simple to tell the two apart. Slowly, every absolute rule I formed always found an exception, and it was quickly apparent that I was no longer safely on the fringes of black and white but would have to start embracing all the gray.

We are idealistic until we're forced to pay attention. Viewing life simplistically most likely comes from all the TV and movies we see, where everything seems to be so perfect, nobody ever talks over each other, and everything has a clear and satisfying outcome. When we're in the safety of the school system, most of our idealisms are reinforced, because we're in a controlled environment. If you bring cupcakes to class, make sure there's one for everybody. If there's a problem, tell a teacher or other responsible adult. Playing by the rules is the only way to get ahead. But once we're in the real world, those absolutes go out the window, and we have to start looking at the finer details and complexities of life.

The irony isn't lost on me of following up a section titled "Zoom Out" with one titled "Zoom In." They're both important steps, and knowing when to do one over the other is the talent that's going to help us take life in the direction we want to go. The devil's in the details, but so are the angels, and you're too smart to float through life oversimplifying things that deserve much more attention.

Observing life on a deeper level will help us understand ourselves better. Our motivations, longings, intentions can all find clarity when we notice the patterns that have always flowed through existence. That clarity robs us of the luxury of being judgmental and simplistic. We may discover that even bad people are more complex than we thought and that people we vilify are not much different from us. I'm not telling you to condone bad choices or bad behavior, but I am suggesting that by better understanding people, we may be able to prevent bad people from doing bad things.

Zooming in will allow us to immerse ourselves in things on a level that helps us develop empathy for others, which* helps us develop more empathy for ourselves. Knowing there's more beneath the surface inspires us to dig deeper and not react prematurely, giving us time to gain more understanding.

Taking a closer look at ourselves also helps us to separate ourselves from anomalous choices we make and behaviors we pursue so we don't tattoo them onto our identity and self-worth. This will free us from the burden of a lot of unnecessary regrets, like beating ourselves up over the dumb shit we all inevitably do.

It'll rarely ever be all or nothing, and there's so much in between that deserves exploring. This exploration allows us an infinite number of new perspectives that will serve us well as we deal with the increasing number of challenges life throws our way.

So, suspend your judgment and take a closer look; marvel at the details and complexities that situations in life present. Who knows what you'll find?

---

* I know I sound like a broken record.

20

LIFE ISN'T BLACK AND WHITE, THERE'S PLENTY OF GRAY IN BETWEEN

When I was in my twenties, I didn't think it was possible to make a best friend as an adult. Most of the guys I hang out with I've known since elementary school, but I started longing for a friend who could relate to the side of myself that inspires my art. My childhood friends still saw me as just Kanwer, Kman, or the other list of words they used to make fun of me.

Through my journey as an artist I started coming across more like-minded people. And one of those people became a very close friend, very quickly.

This friend spoke only with passion, and the word *realistic* was blasphemy to him. He saw making art as a privilege and took it very seriously. He reinforced the importance of a good work ethic and set a good example: man, he worked! We'd go for walks and plot and scheme about our future as artists, but beyond that, we worked.

A rapper by the name of Tony Yayo said in an interview, "Look man, if I can't afford two, I'm not buying one," and that inspired us to have a "two of everything" mentality. I was healing from the worst heartbreak I'd ever experienced and didn't want to give my heart out to another girl. So instead, I gave it to him, my brother from another mother.

I was sick of all the bad people, the shady people, the greedy people. I wanted to be around good people, and he was good people. He cared about me, he paid attention to me, and he did something that at that point no one had done for me before: He made my problems his.

Two of everything.

If I hated someone, he hated that person too. If I was struggling, he sat with me and tried to help me figure things out. He was a guardian angel who smoked too many cigarettes, but our vibes aligned and he was helping me understand myself better.

He was passionate about the art, and he believed I was important. Who doesn't like having someone around who makes you feel like you matter?

When he began to have conflicts with my other friends, I chose him. When his stories contradicted others, I chose him. I chose him every time, even when it didn't make sense. It wasn't even that I wanted to believe him—I needed to.

As we journeyed together in the art world, business got involved, and then he borrowed some money from me that I couldn't afford to give him. The time to repay came and went. He assured me he would handle things and make things right.

His excuses for the indefinite delays were lame, full of holes, and increasingly unlikely. But none of that was a match for my denial. My denial was bulletproof; reality could not pierce that armor. I was already in too deep; believing him gave me optimism, and optimism felt good. I ignored a lot of people's advice.* Even when a friend showed me some irrefutable proof of my friend's lies, I still didn't believe it and had to ask him for myself.

So I called him and asked about the inconsistencies in the stories he'd been telling me. He immediately hung up, and I never saw or heard from him again.

I didn't think it was possible that a dude could break my heart, but he did.

I trusted him, cared for him, gave him my time, love, attention, and energy, and he threw it away with lies, manipulation, and outright disrespect. This put a huge strain on me as a person, and on my bank account.

But this type of heartbreak didn't make me cry; it made me mad. I was mad at him for being a bad person, and even more mad at myself for not seeing all the deception as it was happening. I felt victimized and carried myself accordingly, looking for any opportunity to soak up some pity points from anyone who would listen. I started to think and talk about him as The Bad Guy, the guy who was selfish, manipulative, and weak. I, obviously, was The Good Guy, the guy who was innocently trusting and a good friend all along the way.

As time went on, and more details emerged about him and his pattern of behavior, I realized I wasn't the first person he had lied to, and I definitely wouldn't be the last. He had created a pyramid scheme for himself where he took money from one person to give to another—but all to keep himself afloat. When he couldn't get money from someone else to give to me in time, he ran.

At first, I had no sympathy for him. Thanks to him, I now owed money to other people. I told those people that I didn't have what I

---

* I would eventually have to hear "I told you so" so many times.

owed them, and I wasn't sure how I was going to get it, but I was going to make it happen one way or the other.

That's not an easy thing to tell people. Most people want to avoid conflict and uncomfortable situations. But the more I learned about my former friend, the place he had come from, and the tools he was missing for dealing with challenges, the less I saw a devious person rubbing his hands together laughing at those he betrayed. Instead, I began to see someone afraid of coming clean and piling up more lies to keep the original ones afloat. That's a challenging situation for anyone to be in, and although I don't think he made the right decisions, I also don't see him, or his choices, as the spawn of Satan.

He wasn't The Bad Guy—**he was afraid and made choices that made things worse.**

I've been afraid before, and I've definitely made choices to avoid facing those fears, and those choices made things worse for me as well.

After looking closely at the situation, I had to take ownership as well. I wasn't The Good Guy all the time. I didn't do any due diligence on this new friend, and I'd rejected the advice and care of my other friends in the process. Moreover, I'd let my excitement about a new person who was so unwaveringly supportive of my work get in the way of my judgment. I had been generous beyond my own capacities in part because I liked how he made me feel. I wanted him to like me, and had I been more honest with myself about what I could and couldn't afford, I could have avoided the whole situation.

When I came to that realization, my resentment began to fade.* Playing the victim was also tiring and began to make less sense. I

---

* Though very slowly.

realized that one of the many gifts he had given me was leaving my life, but not before showing me some valuable truths about myself.

He could have spoken to me about the hole he was digging himself into, and I would have wanted to help him, but he didn't, and I'll never know why—but it doesn't matter now. More than a dozen other people in my life deserved my energy more than he did, and this experience only brought me closer to those wonderful individuals in my life. The challenges that came from that whole ordeal made me significantly wiser and stronger, and in many ways gave me a reason to start writing about the lessons I was learning in life.

It's convenient and lazy to label things as good and evil, people as The Bad Guy and The Good Guy. It doesn't require much understanding, just a firm judgment. But when we zoom in a bit closer and examine the details, we realize that things aren't as black-and-white as we thought, and there's a lot of gray to explore. In the short term, I was hurt and betrayed, but in the long term, I found the opportunity to grow and evolve from the difficulties I faced in this situation.

We have that option with every challenge that comes our way. **We just have to hold off on our judgment, try to gather more information, and gain a better understanding of what's happening.** It's okay to have emotional reactions—we're all human. Let's just be mindful of our initial reactions and give ourselves some time to sort things out.

The collateral tragedy when we're betrayed isn't what someone stole from us, or even the damage they did to our heart; it's the idea that we may not trust again. A horrible situation can turn an open and loving person into a cold, hardened version of their previous self, hiding in a shell of trust issues and resentment. This was not what I wanted.

Although I've never received an apology, and it took a few years, I've forgiven my former friend. Not because what he did was acceptable, but because to heal from it and move on, I had to let it go. The warning signs were there, and that experience has saved me a dozen times from similar situations. All the money I lost I now consider tuition, and the scars on my heart, though healed, have left marks as reminders to pay attention not to what people say, but rather to what they do.

In the swamp of lies he told, there was one truth that I was able to see once I took a closer look. He really did believe in my talents and saw me as a vehicle to take him to where he wanted to go, and that's morbidly flattering—completely flattering, in fact, had it not motivated his efforts to exploit me. I had entered the friendship with the idealistic thought that anyone who saw the magic in me would instantly be inspired and help me. That's what I saw on TV, after all—people got discovered and then experienced their big break! Any problems that existed between friends would resolve themselves in twenty-two minutes with some corny dialogue. Things always worked out in the end; good people had good things come to them, and things were "meant to be." Resentment never built up, and all was forgiven and reset before the next episode began.

What happened instead is that I learned that many of the people who see your magic are going to find ways to exploit you for their own benefit. Zooming in made me realize that as much as this person took advantage of me, he also saw talent in me. When I stripped away the black-and-white lens of good and bad and paused to look at the situation with less judgment, I was able to see the positive part of a person who had hurt me. Still, I'd learned a valuable lesson: Don't hold grudges against people who wrong you, and steer clear. Continue on your journey with people who care about you and your purpose.

There is no absolute good and bad; everything is what we make of it. As we strive to understand more than we evaluate, we open up more possibilities and opportunities for things to improve and unfold the way we want them to. This requires paying attention, and allowing a situation to be complicated, and sorting through the details—zooming in—to find where all the magic is hiding.

I aim to see all the gray I can so I can better understand any challenge that comes my way. Having compassion for others during their challenging times has allowed me to have more compassion for myself. That compassion is what allows me—and can allow you—to see all the hidden beauty and opportunity life has to offer.

THERE IS NO ABSOLUTE
GOOD AND BAD;
EVERYTHING IS WHAT
WE MAKE OF IT.

21

DON'T BE SO HYPERBOLIC

(THAT'S A BIG WORD FOR DRAMATIC)

When I was ten years old I went to a local arena to ice skate with my fifth-grade class. My parents couldn't buy me skates, so along with the other kids without skates, I ran around the rink playing tag, avoiding the kid who was "It." As I was running from the It kid, I set off a chain of events that would change my life forever.

I was running and looking back at the kid when the arm of my jacket got caught on a loose nail. You know when you watch a cartoon, and the characters are driving and make a sharp turn by grabbing onto a light post and swinging on it? That's pretty much what happened to me, but I was turning directly into the boards. When you watch hockey, you'll notice there are boards starting at the ice, then glass starting around the height of a hockey player's chest. Or in this case, mouth-level for a ten-year-old boy.

I swung into the boards mouth first. I hit them so hard I saw stars.

I woke up surrounded by other kids. One kid said, "Are you oka . . . oh wow."

All the kids gasped as they stared at my mouth. I moved my tongue forward, only to realize that not much was there to block it from hitting my lip when my mouth was closed. A friend held a tiny mirror to my mouth, and it looked like I had two very crooked fangs.

My front teeth had been cracked, leaving very little behind.

This cannot be happening! This is not real!

Cue the tears.

When you're a kid, it's usually the reaction of the people around you that determines whether you should cry or not. The shock and disbelief on the other kids' faces set off the waterworks.

I was freaking out. I had no front teeth, my lips were bruised and bleeding, and I was scared I was going to get in trouble. None of the teachers could hide their shock once they saw me. After spending a few years as a teacher myself, I now know they were probably very worried about getting sued for what happened under their watch.

They called my dad, who drove a cab in the area at the time, and he picked me up and took me straight to the dentist. The dentist gave me temporary caps and scheduled surgery for a few days later. My parents weren't mad, and I wasn't as scared anymore, but I also realized those were my adult teeth, so I wasn't going to grow any new teeth.

I had root canal surgery, and the dentist filed down the two fangs and molded permanent crowns on top of them. Suddenly I had big buck teeth, too big for my face. They were so bright and white and stood out a bit too much. The dentist told my parents I would grow into them, but at that moment, I pretty much looked like a beaver.

You've probably noticed them peeking out of my beard on the back of this book.

This experience was overwhelming and traumatic for me and was the most catastrophic thing I'd ever experienced in my young life. I remember looking into a mirror trying to figure out whether I could live without front teeth. At the time it felt like losing a limb.

When I take a closer look at what happened, losing my teeth wasn't the end of the world. Often, when bad things happen to us, we freak out. But what does that help us accomplish? I found myself only more and more afraid, which didn't help anything at all. Ten-year-old me never calmed down. I was teased about my big front teeth, but that still didn't confirm my fears that life was over. Life continued.

When I reflect on the experience as an adult, I realize that good things came from losing my front teeth. The most important of those good things was the realization that I survived what felt like a major catastrophe for ten-year-old me. At the end of the day, it wasn't a catastrophe that required surviving; it was just a situation that didn't require overreacting. Oftentimes, how we handle something matters more than what actually happened. This experience taught me to be mindful of that with future challenges.

It wasn't the last catastrophe I faced in life; it was just the beginning of the rollercoaster. Just when you finally recover from one disaster and think you can handle anything that comes your way, someone kicks you in the teeth.[*]

As Mike Tyson fantastically summed it up, "Everyone has a plan 'til they get punched in the mouth."

When we get punched in the mouth, we freak out. Our plans go awry. Normal suddenly changes. **But overreacting isn't going to solve the problem—overreacting usually becomes the problem.** Instead, figure out how to take things in stride, and let time do its work. For me, the process of healing and coming to terms with the fact that I was going to have fake front teeth forever was foreign to me, but I got used to the idea, just like I'll get used to any other major change in my life.

---

[*] Or in my case, you run face first into the boards on a hockey rink.

When I stopped overreacting about having fake front teeth, I realized that everything has a silver lining, even the most traumatic experience of my short life. With my new fake front teeth, I could dig into a scoop of ice cream and not feel a thing. Ice cream always hurt my teeth, but since no nerves were connected to the crowns in my mouth, I could bite into ice cream pain-free.

We don't need to be so dramatic and hyperbolic about everything. Worrying rarely helps anything, and freaking out usually does more damage than good. We need to acknowledge that trauma is an individual experience for everyone, but let's also be mindful of how often we overamplify the degree of our traumas while underestimating our resilience. Nothing is the end of the world until it's the end of the world, and then nothing will matter anyway. I learned this perspective after taking a closer look at the time I lost my front teeth; we all have our own version of that story.

This is the point of the story where I'm supposed to poetically tell you that every time I look at my front teeth I'm reminded of my resilience and ability to handle any challenge—but that didn't happen. My buck teeth stay tucked beneath my moustache, and I have to overly smile just to show them to the world. New challenges find their way to me, and I go through the same internal struggle and bellyaching for a bit before regaining my composure, zooming in to the situation, and figuring out the healthiest next steps.

NOTHING IS THE END OF THE WORLD UNTIL IT'S THE END OF THE WORLD, AND THEN NOTHING WILL MATTER ANYWAY.

22

DETACH YOUR SELF-WORTH FROM YOUR CHOICES

When I was an elementary school teacher in my former life, one of the coolest and most insightful things I got to do on the road to teaching was complete my student teaching at my old middle school in Rexdale, a neighborhood in the northwest corner of Toronto. It's one of the most diverse parts of the city, and considering that Toronto is one of the most diverse parts of the planet, I felt lucky to be there.

When I say the community is diverse, I don't mean from just an ethnic perspective. The people in Rexdale represent a diversity of beliefs, lifestyles, and economics, and all of that affected me during my formative years. Returning as a student teacher was my opportunity to give back.

Diversity is great, but it also has its challenges. During the first half of my student teaching I was working with first-graders, many of whom weren't able to spell their own names yet. There were academic and behavioral differences among the students, and managing all of that while trying to complete a lesson (under supervision) was daunting. The first-graders were sweet, and I could see that many of the things they struggled with came from home. I was only twenty-two at the time, and some of the parents of these six-year-olds were younger than me. Many of the parents were also single mothers—who had had children when they were still kids themselves—which created challenges for me as a male elementary school teacher.

The real challenges came in my second semester when I moved up to the sixth grade and taught students with IEPs.* Although these kids are the same age as everyone else, they need tailor-made programs, usually at lower grade levels, to accommodate gaps in their abilities and learning. Students aren't held back, because that would negatively influence their socialization, so instead, they are given modified programs to match their academic level. In the class I worked with, I had students who could read complex novels and others who were still using picture books. The teacher's challenge is providing a lesson that engages all the students despite their different levels of learning—in other words, trying not to overwhelm the struggling students or bore the stronger students.

Not all IEPs were for academic ability in my sixth-grade class. I had a student who was on an IEP to address his behavioral issues, because they were negatively affecting him academically. To say it bluntly, this kid was acting wild, disturbing the class any chance he got, and threatening violence toward students and teachers. He was often removed from class to give the other students an opportunity to learn in a safe environment, but again, the goal was to modify a program for him, not isolate him from everyone else.

A counselor who worked with the kid a few days a week developed a red card system. If the student felt angry and was about to have an episode, he held up a red card, and the teacher would grant him a pass to go outside and cool off. Likewise, the teacher had a red

---

* Individual education plans.

card, so if the kid was getting out of hand, the teacher held the card up, signaling the kid to go walk it off.

It was a noble strategy, but the first time I held up my red card, after trying to get the kid to stop disturbing the class, he told me to fuck off and that his father would come kick my ass. I stood there waving that red card like a World Cup referee, but the kid was too upset to honor the agreement.

When his homeroom teacher found out, that teacher addressed him in a way I hadn't seen before. He sat the kid down and said: "I like you, man, but I don't like your choices. I need you to leave those choices at home, or better yet, throw them away, because those choices are hurting a great guy."

The homeroom teacher successfully separated the student from his actions, something counterintuitive in a world where we're so quick to label. He wouldn't call the kid a bully; rather, he addressed the bullying as a choice the kid could stop anytime. This allowed the kid not to feel attacked; the decisions he made were isolated, and he was challenged to rethink his choices.

I began to use that technique on my students, and eventually on myself.

I'm not an asshole, but I can choose to be an asshole, and when I'm an asshole, I can choose to let those actions go and make things better. This perspective is more fruitful than simply saying, "I'm an asshole, this is who I am and who I'll be forever."

We have the opportunity to reverse the momentum of our behavior at any moment. I'm not saying this will be easy, but just taking a deep look and recognizing patterns of unpleasant behavior in yourself is an amazing first step that so few people can or want to take. We can separate ourselves from the poor choices we make and start fresh with better decisions, no self-loathing required.

Most often when we're dealing with our short-term gratification monkey, we're talking to our inner child of sorts, so let's spend less time judging and shaming that child and more time empowering that child to make better choices.

With that disruptive student in my class, we were also very mindful of how we gave him directions. Instead of saying, "You need to stop talking during class," we said, "You need to start paying attention and keeping quiet during class."

The result is the same, but the language packages it differently. Giving students specific actions to *start*, to work on, creates a positive framework for them to improve their behavior without suggesting that something inside them needs to be shut off—to be *stopped*. We can also do this with ourselves.

Instead of saying, "I need to *stop* procrastinating," we can say, "I need to *start* my work."

The first message throws us into a brick wall, but the second empowers us to start something and see progress.

We can try to STOP fucking around, or we can try to START making things better. Doing one still prevents the other from happening—that's the duality of this.

Shifting our perspective to focus on what we need to START doing to improve things will generate much better results for us in life. So many of us define ourselves by our stories, and knowing we can shift ourselves from poor decisions to better decisions is very empowering and allows us to define ourselves by our present, and not be held back by the baggage of the past.

This means **we also need to be kinder to ourselves**. All the guilt and self-loathing we place on ourselves is toxic. The negative self-talk is powerful and not an effective way to get us back on track. We have to remember: The part of us that wants immediate gratification is our inner child, and we need to speak to that child with the same level of love and compassion that we would speak to any child.

We're all going to make horrible choices, but that doesn't make us horrible people. When we zoom in and look at a horrible choice in isolation, it may simply be an outlier, a lapse of judgment, because of many things. **We weren't born out of the box with the right tools to handle life's challenges; we need to learn them,** and we can't demonize those who were never taught better ways of handling things.

What choices can you leave at home that have been leading you down a toxic path? What choices can you start exploring to find a better journey?

WE CAN SEPARATE
OURSELVES FROM
THE POOR CHOICES WE MAKE
AND START FRESH WITH
BETTER DECISIONS,
NO SELF-LOATHING REQUIRED.

CLOSE

There's convenience in being vague. It allows us to make absolute statements like "NOTHING ever goes my way" or "Things are AL-WAYS going bad for me" or "Things are NEVER going to get better." Hearing those absolute and hyperbolic statements is usually the first indicator that we need to zoom in and take a deeper dive into what we're looking at. The challenge is that the details are inconvenient, especially if we want to be emotional, so instead of aiming to have a better understanding, we end up making blanket statements in a fit of emotion.

This becomes an issue if we want to feel better about our lives.

Pausing for a moment and taking a closer look at a situation or people will give you a lot of clarity. While you're pausing, you'll have to suspend your judgment until you have more information, and I've been politely poking that theme into the back of your head throughout this book. When we zoom in, we can better understand the intentions of others, and of ourselves. Often, we don't even know what drives us to make the decisions we make, and taking a closer look can reveal patterns in behavior we want to correct.

Life isn't simply good or bad, black or white, right or wrong; it's a spectrum. Just like hot and cold, there are varying degrees to the things we judge, and the closer we look, the more specific those degrees become. This can, however, turn us into painfully neutral people who see the gray in everything, and the world we live in requires people to sometimes take sides. So we can take a stand, but as individuals, we must see all that exists between the black and the white. This empowers us to explore unlimited potential and opportunities.

If things were only good and bad, we'd have to judge ourselves accordingly, and we are far too complex to be reduced to something so simple. We can be good people who make bad decisions. Lord knows I have and will continue to do so, yet that's how I learn and improve as an individual. I'm able to separate myself from my poor choices—not to absolve myself of the responsibility that comes with them, but rather to avoid tattooing a label onto my forehead based on isolated incidents. When we can do that for ourselves, then we can also do that in relation to others. That level of compassion is needed if we're going to continue sharing this planet with our fellow humans.

In an age when clickbait is rampant and people think that reading an outrageous headline qualifies them to speak intelligently on any topic, we need to bring back actual understanding. It may not be convenient to read a whole article when it feels like the headline suffices, but it's essential. In the same way, it's important to formulate our own opinions instead of simply listening to gossip or other people's sides of a story. The more information we have, the better we can formulate an informed opinion. How we judge the world is a reflection of how we judge ourselves, and vice versa, so let's take an extra breath, pause, zoom in, and not be afraid to scratch at life, the world, others, and ourselves to go beneath the surface.

HOW WE JUDGE THE WORLD IS A

REFLECTION OF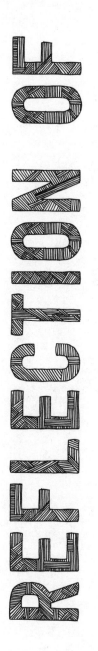

HOW WE JUDGE

OURSELVES.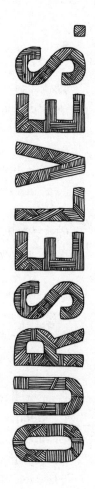

Exit

I look closer at my sadness and I see smiles
I look closer at my steps and I see miles
Between the good and bad I found a spectrum eternal
An infinite journey in gray areas, I've been too scared to explore
It's so convenient not to pay attention
I was quick to judge, slow to learn, not to mention
Cutting no slack
Giving all flack
As if I was absolutely right every single time

Blurry vision kept me from filling the gaps

And all I needed was a breath or three to bring clarity
So comfortable with the doldrums, felt like we were married

I leaned in to peek within
I stepped out to peek around
Disruption and enlightenment were all I found
A fresh start, when I take apart or break apart
Walk away from the rubble
Or decipher it's art

A slight tilt forward, and a breath or three
Shows me the beauty beyond myself
Beyond my life, beyond my death
I'm free

LIMIT YOUR SELF-PITY

Enter

My anxieties are more familiar than my friends
We're so close, they can finish my sentences
So much stacked against me
My bad days don't take a day off
And I have to suffer in silence
Because MY pain is a foreign tongue to everyone else
They wouldn't understand if they tried
And they don't try
Their silence screams
Dousing me in indifference
Why does everyone else get to be better off?
Why does everyone else get to be so happy, it blinds them to me?
Why does everyone else deserve that, and I'm not good enough?
What did I do to deserve the short end of the stick, am I really that
    pathetic
Suffocating behind a silhouette smile
Heart so cold, it's left the rest of me numb
Flames give no warmth, but still burn me
Better off alone, I know how to be lonely

OPEN

The Five S's we have to worry about are salt, sugar, sitting, social media, and self-pity. All are highly addictive, and all will take a heavy toll on us if we consume them over a long period of time.

Self-pity isn't something only lame people do—it's completely understandable. All of us want to feel a connection, and when we decide that no one understands what we're going through, we find a way to connect with ourselves. That need for connection is normal, but there are more sustainable ways to approach it. Feeling sorry for ourselves pits us against others and further isolates us, creating a cycle where we feel we have no one else but ourselves. It's a cycle we can break only when we recognize the toll it takes on us. Yes, it's easy and convenient to always take our own side, and trying to connect and empathize with others takes work, but that's what makes it worth the effort.

When things got difficult for me, I naturally painted myself as the victim, hoping to receive some attention and compassion from others, and it worked. What I didn't realize is that other people could take only so much before my energy became draining. We all have friends who act like Eeyore, constantly moping and complaining about how the universe has conspired against them, and over time, we find ourselves not wanting to be around them as much. This only reinforces their belief that they're on their own, making them double down on their self-victimization.

Power and blame go hand in hand, so if we want to find the power to improve our situation, we're going to have to take responsibility, no matter how much others did us dirty. Taking the time to see how we contribute to our unfortunate circumstances is the first step to turning things around. Comparing ourselves to others and spending excessive time on social media only fuels our self-pity, and the more aware we are of those triggers, the better off we'll be. Pointing fingers and taking offense are also the language of self-victimization, and we need to recognize when this becomes a habit we can't kick. The secret to dealing with much of the bullshit life throws us is self-sufficiency, which means finding ways to own the bullshit, even when there are plenty of other people who should be sharing in the blame.

We create a double standard when it comes to bad news; that isn't applied when things go our way, and we'll benefit from noticing this. Self-pity fuels our insecurities, which in turn bring us more unpleasant feelings of bitterness, anger, and jealousy and a slew of other characteristics we don't want to own.

I said to LIMIT our self-pity, because no one will ever be absolutely free of it. Even when we're feeling down on ourselves, it's okay to take time and feel what we feel; let's just be mindful not to make choices that might make things worse. Choices like broadcasting our self-pity to the world only end up feeding the downward spiral. Sometimes it's better to take a deep breath, give it a few hours, and think about our next move. I've had a bird poop on me before and experienced other random occurrences of bad luck, but I've also found $20 in a jacket I forgot about and was at the right place at the right time to get a great parking spot at the mall. Let's reserve our judgments of the randomness that is life, and when we do, other opportunities, hidden just beneath the surface, will present themselves.

CAUTION: SOCIAL MEDIA IS A PLAYGROUND FOR SELF-PITY

It was odd. I used to work two jobs, one as a full-time teacher and one as a tutor working four hours every night, and I still found time to squeeze in a few hours of creativity before going to bed. I assumed that once I left those other jobs, I'd have more time to get more done, but when I started working as an artist full time, it felt like the opposite.

Throughout my life, I've had that habit of meeting people who I thought had so much more going for them than I did and then taking an inventory of myself and feeling like I came up short. If I met someone with a great body, I'd get down on myself about not spending enough time at the gym. If I met someone with a lot of money, I'd look at my own situation and try to figure out why I wasn't doing more. I'd even start feeling insecure around guys who tied their turbans with cleaner-looking layers than mine. Without fail, every time I met someone, I'd use them as a measure to identify gaps in my life.

Then came social media, the tools where you come across dozens of people every day who make you feel like you ain't shit.

I'd scroll endlessly, watching everyone live their best lives while I was stationary in what felt like every statistical category that mattered. People had more money than I had, they had a healthier dating life than I had, they had clearer skin, more time to come up with a cool Halloween costume, and cuter kids—and I didn't even have* kids!

I eventually got to a point in life where my efforts were paying off. I had things to look forward to, and there was relative peace in my life. Still, picking up my phone and seeing a picture of somebody else, often someone I barely knew, doing something cool left me feeling like I wasn't enough. I'd start to feel sorry for myself and get defensive toward my invisible internal judgmental audience. I'd catch myself belittling other people to try to make myself feel better.

We all want to feel like we're enough, but who gets to decide how much is "enough"?

I eventually had a wake-up call. I was shooting a weeklong music video during which we worked twelve- to sixteen-hour days. I was both in front of and behind the camera, serving as writer, codirector, and star of the project. I would get home, try to get things ready for the next day, and then fall into bed for a solid four to five hours of sleep.

It was awesome.

It wasn't awesome simply because I was delusional from sleep deprivation; it was awesome because I was staying busy, being productive, and working toward something I was excited about. If I could, I would live on set. On set, everyone has a job, and they do it well, and your main responsibility is to focus on your tasks and help others

---

* Or want.

when they need it. It kept me busy, it wasn't too complicated, and I was having a lot of fun.

When the shoot was over, I got to sleep in, wake up in the afternoon, take my time rolling out of bed, and enjoy a day of doing nothing.

But then it suddenly all went downhill.

Did a meteorite crash into my bedroom? Did the stock market, and democracy, crash? Was *The Simpsons* canceled? No, I checked my phone. And I saw someone doing something cool on social media, and I got triggered back into existential dread, feeling like a useless consumer of oxygen.

But I just put in some serious hours working on a very cool project! Doesn't that count for something? Don't I deserve a day to do nothing?

That's when I realized it wasn't the fact that I was having a lazy day. It was the fact that social media would always help me find reasons to feel like I wasn't good enough, even when I was working at my limits.

That's when I decided things needed to change. I needed to get off social media.

You can't quit social media; you have hundreds and thousands of followers! It's literally the only reason why people know you exist and mess with you. It's how you make a living!

That's when I decided things needed to change a little less. I needed to *reduce* my social media.

Drugs like cocaine give you a high, but slowly, your tolerance for the drug increases such that you need more and more to get high, and eventually the drug blows a hole through your brain. Social media is much more vicious because it tickles your reward centers just enough to keep you micro-dosing for more gratification. Maybe it's a like, or a comment, or follow, or just a new picture of your crush, or that person you don't like but have to keep tabs on. In addition to its addictive nature of baby dopamine shots, social media also shows you so many manufactured moments of other people's lives that even the brightest and wisest among us begin to compare fake highlights with the unsexy behind-the-scenes of our own lives, giving our self-esteem constant punches to the gut. It's like eating your favorite flavor of ice cream with micro-shards of glass; it's cutting away at you inside, but you can't stop yourself from having another spoonful.

Social media is truly an awesome creation, but I'm not using the word *awesome* in a positive way. Social media may potentially be the tipping point for our species. Social media use has been linked to depression, anxiety, and addiction, and that's even for people like me, who are old enough to remember life before the internet. The impact of social media on people who have known nothing different in their lives is truly formative.

With that said, make sure you follow me @humblethepoet!

I kid. In all seriousness, I don't think social media is the devil. Like everything in life, it's a double-edged sword, and the more we're aware of the edges, the better equipped we are to address that sword.

I didn't quit social media altogether, but I did take them off my phone. I put all my social apps on an old phone I had lying around— the type of phone that's just slow enough that you get frustrated, put it down, and stop playing with it. I plan my contributions ahead of time and share them on a schedule. I still try to participate and interact with people regularly, but I don't do it whenever I'm bored but during a scheduled time. Once I leave the house, I don't have that phone with me, so the option of killing time on my phone is greatly reduced.

Now I'm forced to find joy in other things, like making eye contact with people and having conversations—with my voice.

Reducing my social media usage has made me more aware of how addicted I was to the micro-gratification it gave me, and it has reduced the number of times I beat up on myself. I was no longer falling into the rabbit hole of other people's carefully curated presentations of their lives and then comparing those presentations to the whole of myself—at least not as much as I was doing that before. And I instantly started feeling better.

Comparing ourselves to others often damages our self-worth and demotivates us, creating a downward spiral. I didn't have the discipline to say, "I'll look at my phone less." I had to make environmental changes. Not only did I take social media off my phone, but I also bought an old-fashioned alarm clock, so picking up my phone was not the first thing I did in the morning. I then crafted a routine of making my bed and doing some push-ups before I allowed myself to look at either phone. My plan has been successful 75 percent of the time, and although that's not perfect, it's made me feel better than I felt before.

I'm more mindful about identifying the gaps in my life in relation to other people. My plate is full, and just because I see someone post a cute #CoupleGoals pic, it doesn't mean I need to reassess my entire life and question whether my accomplishments have come at the expense of my personal life. Social media is a playground for our insecurities and self-pity. It not only makes us feel like we're not enough, but it chips away at our confidence, encouraging us to lash out in uninspiring ways. I don't want to feel insignificant in comparison to others, and I don't want to belittle others to make myself feel better, so I took responsibility to reduce how often I expose myself to those triggers, which are highly addictive.

If you've decided you're sick of self-pity, take a good look at your social media use, and then reduce it. The benefits are almost instantaneous. I'm not promising you'll feel like a million bucks every day, but **you'll find fewer reasons to question whether you are enough, because you are.**

Here's to reducing tendonitis in our thumbs!

COMPARING OURSELVES TO OTHERS OFTEN DAMAGES OUR SELF-WORTH AND DEMOTIVATES US, CREATING A DOWNWARD SPIRAL.

24 SELF-PITY IS EASY AND CONVENIENT LIKE FAST FOOD

(AND JUST AS UNHEALTHY)

I got a text message from a friend three time zones away.

"Can you talk?"

I gave him a call, and he didn't spend even a calorie on small talk and dove straight into his problems with his on-again, off-again girlfriend. He wanted me to help him interpret certain text messages and motives behind her decisions. Having met her only once, I couldn't offer much in the way of reading her mind. I didn't know why she had said their relationship was over and then called him back that same night. I wasn't sure whether her text messages were contradicting each other, or why she would go days without contacting him, only to show up at his front door unannounced.

As he continued to share stories and ask questions, it became clear to me that he was frustrated and hurt and wanted to hear something to help him feel better. But I wasn't exactly sure what I could say to make him feel better.

He wanted to hear something like:

She still loves you.

You're too good for her.

Give her another chance.

She sounds toxic.

Man, if she's worth it, make the effort and try to work it out.

But I didn't want to say just anything to pacify him, so I tried to listen and understand as much as I could and asked questions to help him sort out some of the emotions and fogginess he was experiencing.

Is this the first time she's done this?

Do you think you guys can work it out in the long run?

Is this relationship bringing you the peace you want?

Most of my questions were answered with, "You don't understand . . ." and then he'd jump into another story reinforcing what I was slowly figuring out. The situation wasn't healthy, and he needed to divert his attention and focus on something better in his life.

So I suggested he take a trip . . . with his mom.

"Bro, you just need to be around people who love you unconditionally, and who you can let your guard down around. Take your mom on a trip somewhere nice, sit on a beach, put your head in her lap, and just cry this out."

Although he didn't have the love life he wanted, he did have the money to make something like that happen, and I thought he would love the idea.

Instead, he said, "Bro, you don't understand, I can't go anywhere, not right now, just in case she calls."

"Bro, your phone will work in Hawaii; you can still answer the call."

"No bro, I need to be here, in case she wants to see me."

I rolled my eyes at his response but completely understood. Sometimes the pain is so intense, especially during a breakup, that all you want to do is hear the other person's voice. When you don't know what they're up to, your brain runs a million miles a minute creating horrible scenarios about them—maybe they're with someone else, maybe they're over you, maybe they don't miss you, what if you never hear from them again.

After my futile attempts to provide him with actionable ideas that would make him feel better, he thanked me and got off the phone.

We spoke for another hour the next day, and the next, and the next.

It became clear that even when she did come back to him, he still liked to rehash the bad stuff. He continued to bring up how she hurt him in the past and would relive the drama, continuing the on-again, off-again cycle.

I got it, he was hurt, and who doesn't want the pain to stop? But why would he make choices that made things worse, when there were options that would make things better?—or at least keep things from getting worse.

It was because he, like many of us, was addicted to self-pity. He didn't want to solve the problems, because that meant he could no longer feel like the victim. Self-pity is a tricky thing—an addiction like any other, often birthed from our need to connect and bond with something or somebody.

When we feel sorry for ourselves, we decide that no one understands us, and that lets us create a temporary connection to . . . drumroll . . . ourselves. It's one of the most convenient ways to feel a connection—by finding a reason to feel sorry for ourselves.

My friend didn't reject the idea of taking his mom on a trip because he didn't want to hang out with his mom; he did it because he had found comfort in his self-pity and didn't want to leave its familiarity to do something that would help him get out of it.

We could all order salads at McDonald's, but French fries are so addictive. Quick, easy, and cheap choices will always be more appealing than more responsible choices. Self-pity, among other things, is the fast food of connection. It's easier to feel sorry for ourselves than to book a trip or sit down with a spouse and have uncomfortable conversations.

It didn't matter whether he was having girl trouble, health issues, work drama, or bad weather—my friend was looking at life as if everything was happening to him, and when he reacted in that way, he was harder and harder to be around.

This was a wake-up call for me as well. I did the same thing when my heart was broken. I complained and complained to anyone who would listen and slowly stopped talking to people who lovingly nudged me to grow past it. I also did it in my work, when I was often addicted to feeling sorry for myself because I wasn't getting where I wanted to go. It took me a while to realize that I was pouring salt into my own wounds just to keep them open so that I could keep extracting self-pity from reliving the pain. I did this not because I was a bad person, but because I was exhausted. It doesn't matter if there are better ways; when we're tired and frustrated, we're going to choose the EASIER way, and just like fast food, self-pity feels great in the beginning, but too much of it over time takes its toll.

I got the sobering reminder that no matter how many books we read, how much money we have, and whatever other privileges we possess, we can still easily choose less sustainable paths because they are easier and more familiar. We always lean toward easy and familiar, especially when the other choices are inconvenient and uncomfortable. All personal growth exists outside our comfort zones, and out there, inconvenience and discomfort are inevitable.

Though we all want to be happy, we all have a stronger desire to feel comfortable and safe, and that's okay. We're not weak or whack for wanting that, but we have to realize that it adds up, and we'll be paying a higher price in the long run.

I've lost contact with that friend, most likely because I wasn't encouraging his self-pity and self-victimization. He probably moved on to people who told him what he wanted to hear and gave him what he wanted to feel: pity.

I've been there, but this experience helped me realize that I don't want to be there for long. Quick, cheap, and convenient sound wonderful in the short term, but in the long run, they just supersize our problems and continue our spiral downward. I can't promise anyone a life free from the bad shit, but I can remind you that **self-pity, as comforting as it is, will only make things worse.**

ALL PERSONAL GROWTH
EXISTS OUTSIDE OUR
COMFORT ZONES, AND
OUT THERE, INCONVENIENCE
AND DISCOMFORT
ARE INEVITABLE.

25 WE DON'T SCREAM "WHY ME?!" DURING THE GOOD TIMES, SO DON'T SCREAM IT DURING THE BAD

I used to have a bad habit that when the going got tough, I didn't get going. I complained. I complained to anyone who would listen, and always painted the picture like I was being singled out. Even when there was no one to directly blame, I would wonder why the universe had it out for me, and what I had done to deserve so much bad luck.

When good things happened, though, I wasn't as introspective or appreciative about it. I felt entitled and always expected things to go as planned, and I'd become moody if they didn't.

Nothing put that more into focus than when I almost got into a serious car accident. I was with my friend Balj, a doctor and father of three, and the driver in front of us thought they could be a hero and take a right turn around a bus from the center lane. The bus to their right started moving, and they had to stop quickly. So we had to stop quickly, and in the sideview mirror I could see a BMW barreling toward us.

Fuck, this is going to suck!

The BMW driver didn't attempt to slow down and instead sped up and took a sharp turn around us, avoiding a very big collision. My heart slowly left my throat and reentered my chest.

From the passenger seat I heard Balj exhale in a big sigh of relief. "If we had gotten hit, that would have suuuuuuucked!"

We've all encountered these near tragic situations. Normally they get our heart rate up for a few minutes, and then we settle back down to worrying about the everyday pointless things in our lives. But this time, I refused to let that happen. I put this moment in the bank, to use it against the next shitty situation that came my way.

When bad things happen to us, we can easily fall into the world of self-pity and play the blame game, but how often do we keep the bullets dodged as reminders of how fortunate we are?

I can't claim that life isn't on my side after experiencing something like that. Having had a previous injury and gone through a year of rehabilitation helps me to realize just how much time, energy, headache, and physical pain that BMW maneuver saved me. Tomorrow I may not be as fortunate, but today I am, and for that I celebrate.

We look up to the sky and scream "WHY ME?" when we get dumped, rejected, or other expectations aren't met. **It's very easy to feel sorry for ourselves since it scratches an important itch that we all need scratching: our need to connect.** The easiest person to connect with is ourselves, and the road of least resistance comes in the form of self-pity. There isn't a human being on this planet who doesn't have that need, but depending on who we are, how we were raised, and the tools we were provided with, some of us have discovered more ways to connect than others.

Ironically, we don't ask WHY ME? when we find our soul mates, get that promotion, or have anything else in life work out perfectly. When that happens, we're just happy things worked out as expected. It's a horrible double standard that we should be aware of, because that awareness will motivate us to either complain less or show gratitude more—maybe both if we're lucky.

Most likely neither my best nor worst days are behind me, and outside of being cautious, the only thing I can do is focus on how I handle those things. **We can turn shit to sugar, but we can also turn sugar to shit.** It all depends on our attitude. The sideview mirror image of a gray sports car swerving around me will forever make the difference, no matter what challenge arrives my way.

What's your BMW?

AWARENESS WILL
MOTIVATE US TO EITHER
COMPLAIN LESS OR
SHOW GRATITUDE MORE—
MAYBE BOTH
IF WE'RE LUCKY.

26 TURN REJECTION INTO INVITATION

Rule number one for trying to navigate in the sunny jungle known as Hollywood is DON'T TAKE IT PERSONALLY, EVEN WHEN IT'S PERSONAL.

Much like my relationship with New York City, I had a very foggy view of Los Angeles: the sun shines, the girls are pretty, and everyone is so damn nice. The only thing is, rarely does anyone mean what they say. After a conversation with someone I felt would be great to meet up and work with, I'd fly out to LA, rent a place, rent a car, and prepare for my meeting, only to get ghosted or get hit with a "let's reschedule." In true hustler's fashion, I didn't let it get me down; I would chalk up the experience to learning a lesson and try again another time.

But eventually, it got me down.

There was a big shot in the music industry I wanted to meet, and she actually said she was excited to meet me. So I planned a trip to LA around her, making extra room in my calendar to accommodate her ever-changing schedule. I was working on some great stuff, and this company could help me out a lot, so I held off releasing my work until we could talk.

Knowing that mainstream music people were digging my work did wonders for my ego and excitement. I felt super validated and thought to myself that they would be my trampoline to the next level: mainstream.

When you're a brown artist, the first people who gravitate toward you are people of your community. That gravitation is more like an asteroid hitting your world than a healthy attraction. Being an artist and coming from a conservative culture doesn't mix well, and you begin to work to form a tribe that "gets you" more than looks like you.

I was a target of a lot of criticism from people who looked like me because they had a bias about what a turban and beard represented, and what such an appearance allowed me to do. If we scratched beneath the surface, the real reason there was conflict was because I was making them uncomfortable by exploring new ideas—things they weren't used to seeing or hearing from someone who looked like me. To protect their nostalgia, they attacked and attempted to discredit me. That didn't bother me so much, because I began to gain ground, connecting with a more mainstream, open-minded community of people who simply judged the quality of my work and saw me as nothing more than a guy with a sexy beard. That was refreshing.

So here I was, feeling like I was going to be further plugged into the mainstream world and all my problems with my own community would go away. All I needed to do was get in a room with these people, play them my work, and the rest would be history.

An hour before the meeting, I received an email asking whether we could push the meeting out by a few weeks.

A few weeks, are you kidding me? You know how much money this trip is costing!? Why would you cancel on me so last minute? Am I really that useless to you?

It wasn't just about the canceling; it was the feeling that I didn't matter to them. The whole week I was anxious that they would cancel, and my worries were validated. I wanted to lash out.

I spoke to some friends, all of whom gave me great advice about how to deal with it.

"This happens all the time, you have to roll with the punches."

"This is how the game goes, peoples' schedules change, don't take it personally."

"There's no make-or-break here, more opportunities will come."

But I was fuming on the inside. We get hurt when people make us feel small, and in Los Angeles, people know how to make you feel small without a hint of aggression. They just passively dismiss you or forget you even exist. This also made me feel frustrated with what felt like a stagnant music career. I wasn't getting as far as I wanted.

I was bummed out, upset, and needed to vent, so I called Dominic "D-trix" Sandoval, one of the hardest working, most creative artists I knew, and vomited out my heart. I was hoping to hear some clever strategy to get this meeting back on.

Instead of providing me with advice, Dom challenged me with a question: "Why are you taking meetings with these people?"

"Ummm, because they could really open doors and put me in places I can't get myself?"

"But what good are you to them?"

"Uhhmmm?"

"What leverage do you have going into those meetings that's going to make them want to even see you?"

"Uhmmm?"

"These people won't make you a priority because you are replaceable."

Ouch.

"Your ultimate leverage is your craft. Stop taking meetings, stop networking, stop trying to cut corners, and get better at what you do. As you get better, your craft will be your leverage, and opportunities will find you. Devote more time to your craft and become irreplaceable."

That was one of those moments when I felt like I was both punched in the chest and kissed on the forehead. Dom was right, I was spending more time playing the game than being an elite artist, and when it didn't pan out, I was feeling sorry for myself. I was already popular enough to be on people's radars; all I needed to do moving forward was get better and better.

The better we get at our craft, the fewer people we compete with, and the more we stand out. The only reason I wanted to have this meeting was to cut corners and save my best work for the big stage, but that's not how it works.

After being honest with myself, I realized it was my feeble ego that needed hugging. If I thought validation from a pro would make everything feel better, it wouldn't. In Hollywood, there will always be someone above you on the made-up totem poles. A more sustainable way to feel better about myself is to do things I'm proud of and find satisfaction in my constant improvement. It takes more work, but it pays off and doesn't depend on luck.

Dom gave me a cold shower during that call, and when you watch his work, you can see his blood, sweat, and tears in everything he does.* He's not afraid of the unsexy, repetitive, mind-numbingly boring practice required to be elite. It's the same as Steph Curry practicing the same shot, over and over and over until it's perfect, then doing it a hundred more times.

If you want to be good, practice so you don't make mistakes.

If you want to be great, practice until you can't make mistakes.

I took Dom's advice and stopped trying to have meetings. I

---

* youtube.com/theDOMINICshow

focused more on the daily grind of refining my skill and putting my-self in positions to do things fewer and fewer people could do. It's a lifelong journey, and it requires nonstop repetition to reinforce what we do.

Anything we want to be great at, we have to practice.

> I fear not the man who has practiced 10,000 kicks once, but I fear the man who has practiced one kick 10,000 times.
> —attributed to Bruce Lee

I don't have control over whether people will keep meetings with me. And we all need to respect that people have their own priorities and things they need to do. I don't gain much holding a grudge, and I'm better off recognizing that although I can't control the outcome of another person's decisions, I do have absolute control over my efforts.

When we shift our focus on our efforts and what we can control, we're more empowered and much less frustrated by things that are beyond our control. I'm not going to promote some fluffy ideas like the Law of Attraction, but once I spent more time sharpening my tools and refining my craft, I got more opportunities and more eye-balls turning my way.

In hindsight, I was being both lazy and impatient and then blam-ing others when I didn't see any progress. We have to be honest with ourselves when we ask, *"Can I give this more?"* And we have to understand that patience doesn't mean waiting around for things to happen—it's respecting the time needed for things to play out.

Now, instead of complaining and looking for sympathy, I con-stantly question my effort and try to figure out where else I have power to improve things on my end.

I'm also proud to say I don't take anything personally, even when it is. Showing compassion for others who may not do what I want has helped me both keep a level head and build compassion for myself, especially when I fall short of my own expectations. My ego is now the passenger and not the driver.

Focusing on what's in my control has given me more than enough to work on, so I'll never be sitting around again complaining about what others won't do for me.

WHEN WE SHIFT OUR FOCUS
ON OUR EFFORTS AND
WHAT WE CAN CONTROL,
WE'RE MORE EMPOWERED
AND MUCH LESS
FRUSTRATED BY THINGS
THAT ARE BEYOND
OUR CONTROL.

27

SELF-PITY FEEDS OUR INSECURITIES

(AND THAT LEAVES US BITTER AND ANGRY)

A few years ago, I was staying with Lilly, and we had gone out to buy groceries. Our list was simple, and we split up to grab the essentials. I was in charge of grabbing the bananas. When I brought back my haul, Lilly looked at the bananas and immediately pulled out her camera.

"What are those?!" she mockingly said pointing to the bushel I brought.

"They're bananas," I replied, confused. I wondered why this moment was being documented.

"They're not even yellow!" she laughed.

"Why would I buy them yellow? They'll turn black before we even get home."

"You eat green bananas?"

"I BUY greenish bananas and let them turn yellow."

"Oh my god!"

And the rest was history.

Lilly documents her days in her vlogs, and she's done so for a few years to the point that she's amassed more than 2.7 million subscribers who follow her daily adventures of trying to drink enough water, get through her to-do list, and make fun of me.

This brief moment in internet history sparked an endless debate among her followers about what color bananas should be when you buy them. I always assumed everybody bought them greenish and let them turn yellow over the week. I learned Lilly gets them yellow and tries to finish them before they turn black. It was a light-hearted debate, and fun to have, but when you're having it in front of millions of people, there are some unintended consequences.

To this day I'm still receiving emails, messages, and posts about green vs. yellow bananas. More people watch her vlogs in a day than anything I make in a year, and because of this, when people hear the name Humble the Poet, it's become more synonymous with green bananas than with any other accomplishment I have to my name.

In the beginning it was funny, and I'd laugh when it came up, but eventually, it started to feel like it was becoming my signature. As if I were an actor who was typecast into one role or catchphrase—like the guy who played Pee-wee Herman or Steve Urkel. To be known for a bushel of bananas rather than for my creative work began to chip at me. If I shared any of my work, a significant number of replies would be about bananas. When I ran into people on the street, it would be about the bananas. Can you guess what messages I found in my inbox? Pictures of bananas. At that point, I felt disrespected and labeled. As if I had dug a hole I'd never get out of.

Why the fuck are they still talking about bananas? I'm doing important work here!

Am I really just a sideshow clown to people?

Is the work I do any good if more people care about green bananas?

What the hell is wrong with people!?

It was tragic to think I was sinking into a silly reputation while I was working so hard to be seen for my work. I was making videos online that weren't connecting. I was pushing them out at a regular rate, hoping to gain some traction. Even with cameo appearances and promotional support from Lilly, I wasn't making much progress. That fire of frustration was fed by this banana thing. It felt like a big step back on a journey that I wasn't making much progress in anyway.

I complained about it to Lilly, who hadn't anticipated things playing out the way they did. She offered to stop filming when I was around and to keep me out of her content if that would make me feel better.

But as with every struggle, nothing anyone else does can make us feel better—not sustainably at least. **Our problems aren't always our fault, but they're still our responsibility.** The problem here wasn't the bananas, or Lilly, or even her fan base. The problem was me, and my insecurities about my work and progress.

At that point, I spent more time blaming others than looking at myself when it came to the discomfort of the situation. The real problem was that this video traveled more quickly than any of my work, and that made me feel like my work wasn't any good.

This situation mirrored my insecurity. When we've spent so much time burying our feelings, the smallest things can trigger us, and everything we've been holding in will all come out in one big explosion.

I had to remind myself that nobody bringing up bananas was saying anything about the value of my work, or my value as a person, and that I don't need to wait until things get better in my career to embrace the lighter side of life. I can do that now.

I'll never be able to control how many messages and pictures I get about bananas, and that initially felt tragic and overwhelming. I flirted with the idea of leaving the digital world for good to avoid it. In essence, I wanted to run away.

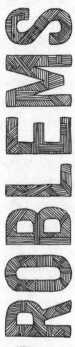

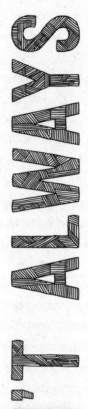

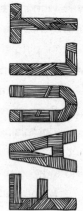

OUR PROBLEMS AREN'T ALWAYS OUR FAULT,

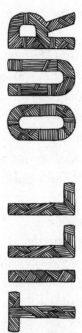
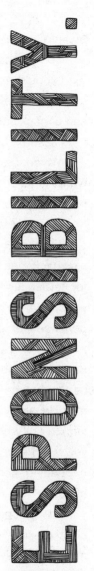

BUT THEY'RE STILL OUR RESPONSIBILITY.

For a guy named Humble, it's ironic how easily my pride could be bruised, just like a banana.

So I wondered, *How should I handle this?*

I should run. But instead of running away, I should run toward it, look it in the eye, and let it reflect all my doubts and insecurities so I can unpack and address them.

I asked a better question: *Where's the opportunity here?*

My goal as an artist is to connect, and if a younger audience wants to tease me about bananas, instead of rolling my eyes, I should play along.

So I started #TeamGreenish.

The reason comedy is so important to life is that it brings joy, but it also packages the truth in a way we can share, and nobody resents us for it. Discussing anxiety, regret, heartbreak, and other abstract ideas will always be a task, and it depends largely on the other person's experiences for me to be able to connect with them on that level.

After #TeamGreenish came into being, whenever I bought bananas, I shared a picture on social media, triggering a storm of debate as to whether the bananas were even safe to eat. Many people took my side, and just as many argued the opposite. People began sending me color charts, and I comedically referred to all things green as yellow, to everyone's delight. I discovered that embracing what was happening, although not ideally what I wanted, had a lot of positive effects.

The people who engaged with my banana arguments also checked out my other work. In many ways, it made the other work more accessible to them because they knew something a bit more normal about me. No longer was I this abstract artist clouded in an air of mystery. Now I was a regular guy who came up with dope ideas and made controversial decisions about bananas.

Everything didn't magically work out, my videos didn't start doing any better, but I did realize that the two weren't related. It wasn't as if the audience wanted me to abandon the topics I passionately discussed to talk bananas; it's just that some content is easier to digest than others. My eventual solution to the lack of traction I felt I was getting on YouTube was to simply move on and away from it and devote my time, love, and energy to things that really excited me.

We fall into cycles of despair, and when we do, we can interpret everything as being against us; that's how it becomes a downward spiral. I began to see this banana episode as the root of all my problems. It never was, but it was a convenient target. It's very easy for us to point fingers at everything and everyone beyond ourselves when we struggle. It allows us to connect with ourselves while simultaneously isolating ourselves from everyone else. The problem with this is that it's not sustainable and creates enough tension in and around us that we become very easily triggered by simple things, like bananas.

This is important to recognize in ourselves and others. Sometimes we'll say small things to someone and they'll lose their shit. It's not because they're crazy—it's because whatever we said was the last straw. People walk around collecting moments of stress, and if left unaddressed, stress will pile up until they hit their limit, and then Kaboom! We've all had our own stories of hitting our breaking point and letting the wrong person have it. Those experiences, as unfortunate as they are, also allow us to find compassion when it happens to others.

Look into yourself and try to figure out the big stress that is magnetically attracting all the tiny stresses to feed your volcano. When we address the big ones, the small ones can slide off our shoulders instead of building up into something they don't need to be. If something minor is setting you off more than normal, it may be a sign that the big one is not far behind. **Find a quiet place, get comfortable, and ask the uncomfortable question: "What's really bugging me?"**

Whatever it is, it's important to be the archaeologist and start digging inward to discover what's down there. You'll quickly realize that problems have layers, and many of them don't have other people's names attached to them. This practice of digging deeper and peeling away layers is important as it'll help us find the root of many of our problems—which is usually about fear. Once we have that understanding of ourselves, we'll have a better handle on the world around us, which will make it feel all that more sweet—like a ripe, greenish banana.

I couldn't help myself.

LOOK INTO YOURSELF
AND TRY TO FIGURE OUT
THE BIG STRESS THAT IS
MAGNETICALLY ATTRACTING
ALL THE TINY STRESSES
TO FEED YOUR VOLCANO.

28
GETTING OFFENDED IS A FORM OF SELF-PITY

"Turb, Turb . . ." I was livid. Watching Nicki Minaj refer to Gurpreet as "Turb" on *American Idol* was rehashing all my childhood traumas of being bullied and teased by other kids for having a turban.

It was 2013, and I was watching *American Idol* in my living room. Gurpreet, a Sikh contestant, was trying to win over the judges to send him to Hollywood. He, or the producers of the show, decided it was important that he shared his nickname "Turbanator," followed by a very distasteful CGI rendition of changing the color of his turban as if it were an LED panel. His name went from Gurpreet, to Turbanator, to now just Turb, and he was either fine with it or biting his tongue, not wanting to ruin the chance of becoming an American idol.

When he finished singing, he received two "yes" votes, and one "no," with the deciding vote being Nicki Minaj. In his campaign to swing her vote, Gurpreet pointed out that he also owned a turban the color of her hair. She interrupted him by calling him "Turb." This made the other judges laugh and sent a lump down my throat. All the while, Gurpreet had his hands together begging her for the shot, his dignity out the window.

"Turb, you're going to Hollywood!" she announced as the music began and Gurpreet jumped up and down, more CGI changing the color of his turban to match the music.

Cringe. But I tried to reason.

Fine, they weren't being the most kind and sensitive to him, but it's America, and in the entertainment business, you need thick skin, and he may not even have been aware they were going to CGI colors onto his turban, I can't hold this against him, or them, for not showing a level of cultural sensitivity.

But then it happened.

As Gurpreet came out of the audition room, his family waiting to hear the good or bad news, he pulled his ticket to Hollywood OUT OF THE BACK OF HIS TURBAN. At that point I could no longer justify this emphasis on Gurpreet's turban as creative editing from the show's producers: he was playing along with it.

What type of Stockholm Syndrome did I just witness? This guy just pulled a ticket out of his turban!

I paced back and forth in my room trying to make sense of this and contain my rage. I had a decent online following back then and wanted to vent my frustrations by writing a song dissing the show, Nicki Minaj, and Gurpreet, who I felt was acting like an Uncle Tom.

I called Sikh Knowledge, who makes much of my music, and told him we needed to start cooking.

"Who the fuck is this guy, and how is he letting them speak to him like this!? Has anyone ever made anything of themselves winning American Idol? What the fuck?! Who the fuck is Nicki Minaj to act like that?—she's Trinidadian and from Queens. She probably grew up with people wearing turbans, how she gon be so disrespectful like that, fuck them all, they need to get it! Doesn't this guy realize he's setting us back fifty years acting like this?!"

Sikh listened patiently and then replied, "Look man, I know you're mad, and if it's as bad as you described it, that's definitely whack, but you're too talented to be acting like this right now. We can make a song and turn this into something more than it already is, or you can do what you've always been doing, making dope art, and let that speak for itself. Do you really want to be remembered as the sensitive guy who attacked Nicki Minaj? I'm surprised you got offended by this; you're too talented and cool to let this shit get to you. Stop feeling sorry for yourself and get back to work."

I opened my mouth, but nothing came out. What could I say? He was absolutely right. Gurpreet's experiences and choices weren't a reflection of me, and going public dissing someone I should consider a brother was more about me gaining attention than about having important conversations and resolving anything. I never made music attacking people, so why start?

No one can offend us without our permission.

"I'm sorry man, I lost my cool. This pissed me off on a level I didn't know could happen."

"That's okay man, let's just keep making dope shit, and let these clowns fade away themselves."

When we got off the phone, I had a moment of clarity. I looked back at the past twenty-four hours and wondered how I had allowed myself to get so worked up over something so trivial. I began to scan my memory for the last time I was justified in feeling so offended, and nothing registered. **I could not find any utility to being offended; I only felt conquered and controlled.** At that moment I decided that getting offended was no longer for me. I ended it cold turkey. I think the embarrassment I felt from letting someone take hold of my emotions was so strong that I never wanted to feel it again, and I haven't.

Yes, I have not been offended by anything since that moment in 2013. I don't think most life transformations happen cold turkey like that, but once in a while, a bone-headed decision hits us so hard, we get smacked into new priorities.

I continue to experience racism of varying degrees on a regular basis, but I no longer allow it to offend me. For instance, none of the online comments about my work penetrates my skin. Even when a close friend is critical of me, I may spend four minutes getting defensive before regaining my composure, hearing what that friend has to say, and applying it accordingly. My constant mantra on this topic is simply "those who offend you, conquer you." Presidential tweets can elicit an eye roll, but they never make it to my heart, nor will personal attacks or anything else that may have rattled me a few years before.

The internet has made it very easy to tell the world you're offended, and at this point, everyone can find anything offensive. Screaming "I'M OFFENDED!" online is a way of finding people who show you empathy; it's a call to connect, and as much as I can relate to wanting to connect to others, it's not the most sustainable way of going about it.

Feeling sorry for ourselves because someone else did something we don't like, and then proceeding to tell the world about it, isn't the best use of our energy. When I was nine years old, a woman told me she was offended that I came to her country looking the way I did. I was confused because I was born in Canada, but that also set a tone for how ridiculous being offended really can be. I don't hold any ill will toward Gurpreet, or Nicki, or the creators of *American Idol*; they all did what they did in a way they thought best and have to live with the outcomes of those decisions. I did rewatch the moment on YouTube, and it's still very cringey, but I'm glad I didn't let my emotions get the best of me.

I'm proud that that was the last time I got offended. I've had other opportunities to take offense since then, and some people have even directly tried to get under my skin, but I've remained cool—maybe because I have a deep respect for Sikh Knowledge, and I don't want to be lame in his eyes by getting offended. He was also right. All these years later, here I am, publishing my second book with a major publisher and releasing music with international partners, setting a tone for what a guy with a turban can be, grateful for guys like Gurpreet who entered uncomfortable situations so the rest of us won't have to.

THOSE WHO OFFEND YOU, CONQUER YOU.

CLOSE

I once spent a week in bed drowning in self-pity. Sleep was my weapon of choice to deal with the pain, regret, stress, anxiety, and overall weight on my chest. I sometimes still use this coping mechanism, but only for an hour or two, when I'm stressed out and I know that anything else may make things worse. I give myself permission to do this because I noticed a pattern: if I let some time pass, things become easier to manage. I show myself compassion and allow myself that time.

I don't often tell anyone about my challenges because I feel like I may fall into the trap of looking for pity and validation. I'm not sure whether it's right all the time to do this, but sometimes the differences between self-pity and self-compassion are too subtle to notice. **This section is called "Limit Your Self-Pity," not "Learn How to Be a Stone-Cold Stoic Who Feels Nothing."** The goal isn't to encourage you to fight your feelings; it's to help you determine when your feelings are holding on to the steering wheel and are about to crash you into a park full of children.[*]

We're always facing an ongoing balancing act between giving ourselves a hug and a pat on the back and giving ourselves a kick in the butt. We can learn how to improve how we treat ourselves

---

[*] Too much?

through our relationships with others. This took me a while to figure out, because the moment I vowed "no more self-pity," I came out of the gate cold and apathetic toward others. Looking back, that was understandable, and I slowly warmed back up to people. I needed time, we all need time, so let's give ourselves that time.

So in addition to limiting our self-pity, let's work to feed our self-compassion. That can mean anything from taking a me-day off from work, to eating an extra three Ferrero Rochers, to saying "no" to the next ten people who ask for a favor, to walking away from an argument even if we're right because we can't afford to spend the energy. It can be hard to feel compassion toward adults; if someone is rude to us on the bus, we take it personally, rarely thinking about what got that person to their breaking point. So showing compassion for ourselves and compassion toward others goes hand in hand.

Remember the inner child I talked about earlier, the one who knows the world only in reference to themselves and has to learn empathy? Even though they need discipline and teaching, they also need love. I try to see the inner child in everyone, including myself, when I need to muster up compassion in challenging times. If it's a one-time occurrence, it's easier to let it slide off my back. If it becomes a pattern of behavior, then just like with a child, the response has to be elevated so the behavior isn't validated. That's the teacher in me talking, but it works. I'm showing myself compassion by not allowing myself to be in situations that drain me of my energy, attention, love, and time. I recommend you do too, while being cautious not to throw a mask on your pity.

We aren't victims of life—we *are* life. We have power over our efforts, which gives us power to adjust our sails depending on which way things are blowing. Self-pity serves as a barrier to those sails and sets us on a one-way path downward. Our problems may not be our fault, but they are definitely our responsibility, so ask yourself how well excessive self-pity and seeking pity help with that responsibility. The more we exercise our power to turn our days around, the more the tools to help us will find us. Champions have to feel like champions way before they ever raise their hands in that big victory, so remember that you're a champ—and act like it.

Exit

A broken heart can serve as an open heart
Flooding us with pain that lifts us into oceans of misery and
    misfortune
But I could only feel the pain of others, once I recognized the
    pain of mine
We're all in that same boat, acting like we're alone
Like bad luck kicks only our butt
We decide our spiral
Downward or up
It's all up to us
Wait for our turn to speak, or listen to others
I mean listen listen
Puts us in a position to feel others' conditions
And build a connection
I don't want others to feel what I did
But they'll have to feel it to get it
Happiness is a lousy teacher
And I couldn't explain it
But I can accept it
It's not just happening to me
Unfortunate circumstances aren't the enemy
They're opportunities
For bridge buildings and olive branch sharings
And "I know how much that must suck" type of caring
Things don't get better, we'll just get tougher
Stronger, with an open heart, that loves much longer

THERE'S NO WIN OR LOSE, THERE'S ONLY WIN OR LEARN

Enter

Life has taken so much from me, I'm not sure what's left
Love has taken so much from me, I've run out of breath
There's a hole in my soul, and it's leaking my life away
Like an hourglass, covered top, unsure of how much sand remains

OPEN

Bill Gates said it best: "Success is a lousy teacher." If things continued to go flawlessly, there wouldn't be much of a story to tell when we look back. It's the resistance, the heartaches, the disappointments, and the challenges that give life spice, and give us a story worth telling.

When we're in school, things are much simpler. We know who our teachers are, and they tell us what they're going to teach us. We get assessed and evaluated, and we receive just enough validation and acknowledgment to keep trying. Once that school bell rings for the last time, however, we're on our own—but we still have so much to learn. As I stated earlier, it's like leaving the zoo to move into the jungle—sure we're free, but we gotta figure things out on our own now. Not only are the cages gone, so is the zookeeper with our dinner. We graduated to the school of life. Tuition is expensive, and we always pay in advance.

Life is trial and error, and culture is a collection of some of our best practices handed down from generation to generation, but even they aren't one-size-fits-all. We have to make our own mistakes to figure everything out. When we were kids, we had to bump into something before we stopped running in the house; we had to burn our hands before we stopped playing with the stove. And now, we gotta get our assess kicked a few dozen times before we get the hang of whatever the rest of this life is.

We fear losing and failure, but we don't realize that's where all the lessons are hiding. We try something, it doesn't work, we try something else. This method of trial and error has been the foundation of our species and took us from simple cave paintings to selfie sticks. Our progress is paved with mistakes, failures, and defeats, and it's our resilience that keeps us keeping on.

Every misstep is a teacher, and not all the things and people we lose in life end up being losses. Our obsession with winning can cost us much more than losing a healthy outlook when life doesn't go our way.

There's always a lesson, a nugget of wisdom or a jewel waiting when things look like they won't be going in our favor; we just have to be willing to pay attention and do some digging if need be.

Once we remind ourselves to find opportunity in any situation, there is no loss, just learning. Failure isn't the opposite of success, it's a path to it.

Recently, I started receiving offers to consult for companies. I had no idea what consulting was, or how I was qualified. As I dug deeper I realized it had to do with businesses trying to learn an expert's advice, but I was struck by the irony of it: my expertise only comes from experience and making a lot of mistakes. The only way any company is going to learn will be the same way: learning from their missteps. To learn from our losses means we have to abandon our timelines and expectations, and to show patience for the necessary time it takes for things to happen. Chasing shortcuts is often the reason we feel burned by the universe.

Take heart: Losses become gains when we let go of resentment, regret, grudges, and self-pity, because that opens us to finding the value in the times things don't go the way we want. Learning to adjust and adapt opens up the world and ourselves to new experiences and treasure in any trashy situation.

29

STOP CALLING THEM FAILURES, START CALLING THEM TEACHERS

I got a text wishing me a happy birthday from a number I didn't recognize. Turns out it was a friend of my girlfriend at the time, and since she was out of town, she had asked her friend to reach out and deliver my gift.

When we met up, he gave me specific instructions as to which boxes to open first, and my excitement grew. In the boxes were assorted little cute gifts, ones that had more sentimental value than anything. Popcorn toppings, tickets to a concert, and a handwritten letter.

My girlfriend was traveling to a wedding with her family and knew she would miss my birthday, so she had planned this out. I don't remember the details of the letter except it was covered in kisses, and in one part she wrote: "I know we've been having trouble lately, but we love each other enough to make this work. I'm not going anywhere."

That part of the letter made me tear up. There was a lot of tension in our relationship, our schedules didn't match anymore, and we were sneaking around our families. The promise in her letter took a massive weight off my chest, and it felt like the best birthday ever.

SPOILER ALERT: She didn't keep that promise.

Our problems continued, our fights got more intense, and then she asked for a break.

"A break? Did you not read the part of your letter where you wrote that we were going to figure this out? What do you mean break? We'd stop fighting if you'd just let me meet your mom. I have a proper full-time job, and I come from a good family. What's the problem?"

She wanted a break, and I took that as my cue to figure out all the ways I would improve our situation after she caught her breath. I planned heartfelt monologues and cute date ideas. This wasn't going to be a Ross and Rachel "break"; this was going to be a pause before we took things to the next level.

SPOILER ALERT: Things didn't go to the next level.

A few weeks into our break, I called her because I missed her. She explained to me that a week before, she and her mom had been in a car accident. They were banged up; she was going to physiotherapy for her wrist, and her mom hurt her back.

"So you almost died and didn't tell me? Me, of all people?! Shouldn't I have been the first face that flashed in your head as you drove into that ditch?! If I survived a near-fatal accident, the first thing I would have done was broken down your door and proposed!"

But instead, she wanted me to know that the accident had given her time to think, and she didn't want our situation to be a distraction anymore in her life, and that it was over.

But what about that letter?

I sat on the floor crying, trying to reread the letter, but my vision was blurry from the tears. They fell on the page and made her words smudge as well. Nothing made sense. I had it here in writing! She promised that we were going to make it work! Isn't this like a contract and legally binding?

I sniffed the kisses on the page, realizing I might never taste her lips again—nobody prepared me for that. I tore one of the kisses out of the page, and I ate it.

Sitting there on the floor in my room, crying from being dumped, I ate the entire letter. I tore it to pieces and ate each and every piece like it was popcorn, like I was living in the saddest movie I'd ever seen.

When someone ends a relationship with you, the "acceptance" stage of grief is in no rush to greet you. I had been holding on to hope since the break, but clearly, things were going in the opposite direction, and I just ate any physical evidence that I had a chance.

I devoted the next few months to figuring out why everyone else's relationships were working and mine weren't. I wanted to know, "What do they have that I don't?" I wanted to learn something new from them so I'd never have to lose at the game of love ever again. I wanted to know why everyone else deserved to be happy but me.

It was a silent expedition, trying to pick up subtle cues and eavesdrop on phone calls and in-person conversations. I quietly observed friends and family in their various dynamics and made some surprising discoveries.

Not too many couples, after closer inspection, were any better off. They had communication issues, fought proxy wars, and left things unaddressed until everything festered into something bigger. The common thread in their conflicts were unrealistic and unfair expectations—which I'd had, too, when I'd entered my past relationship.

I expected my ex to know what she wanted and to keep the promises she made, when really, I knew she was just as scared and ill-prepared for the relationship as I was. I didn't come to this realization after meditating in the forest or reading a profound message on social media. I truly grasped this idea only when I was the one having to end a relationship. That shit is hard!

It's never easy for anyone to end a relationship, let alone communicate it to an uncooperative partner. My former girlfriend needed to go because she wouldn't have been happy if she had stayed. The true failure would have been being unable to communicate this to me and sticking around to avoid conflict, but she handled it the best way she could with the tools she had.

Although I lost her, I (eventually) gained some very important insights and perspectives on what it means to coexist with another person, and how complex that dynamic can be. It's never as simple as it looks in the movies. **Love isn't the glue, it's the fuel.** And it wasn't her absence of love for me that killed our flame; it was her love for herself that pushed her into a new direction—a direction that I couldn't be a part of.

SPOILER ALERT: She came back, a few times.

But by then it was too late; I had survived the heartbreak and started a new chapter, and she knew she was just tired, clinging to something familiar. We both learned a lifetime of love lessons from each other, and although the intensity of the heartbreak was a heavy bill to pay, we never get to decide the price.

Had we waited any longer, that price could have been even higher; it's pay now or more later, but the price of the lesson was going to get paid. I experienced rebounds after her, but I knew that I wasn't in a position to be serious with anyone else for a long time after her. It would be eighteen months before I entertained anything serious.

SPOILER ALERT: I would have a few more heartbreaks as my story unfolded, each more unique and severe than the last, and who knows, maybe my heart will suffer a crack while I'm writing this book.

Each of those heartbreaks came with a silver lining of life lessons and wisdom I could carry forward with me into the next relationship. I became mindful of patterns in my behavior and desires and started paying attention to how that affected the other half of the relationship dynamic. I went through so many breakups and makeups that I began to stop fearing them.

I realized that with any loss comes gain. If things don't work out my way, the consolation prize is a lesson I can keep close to me for the rest of my life. Those lessons encourage more self-awareness, which in turn strengthens my most important relationship—the one with myself.

The perspective that we win even when we lose has helped me move forward with far less fear than I used to have. It's allowed me to be more open and honest in matters of the heart, and realize that clear communication has been a great friend to me—in my friendships, business relationships, and matters of love. Over time, I've learned to manage my expectations and dependencies when it comes to relationships, and not just the romantic variety.

I learned something else in my little investigation into other couples: All relationships depend on priorities, and I couldn't see whether my priorities matched those of someone else if I didn't know my own.

Relationships don't get easier; we just get more prepared because we become more aware—aware of how we view things, how to look at things in other ways, and how we react when our expectations aren't met.

In the end, I didn't let the heartbreak be a tally on a loss list. I learned a lot and gained so much from it, and found gratitude through the experience. I know future heartbreaks will yield the same, and the process of learning won't always be the most enjoyable. We have to try our best to see how these moments of loss open other doors for gain in life.

That change in perspective has allowed me to move forward without fear of getting hurt, because I know I'll learn and grow from it. This has saved me from wearing trust issues like a badge of honor and closing myself off to a world I enjoy being connected to.

I wish all the best to the ex who led me to eating her love letter. I haven't looked her up on social media or run into old mutual friends. She taught me a lot about who I am and how I can best be in relationships with others, and for that I thank her. Everything that I initially considered a loss from that situation I now see as a blessing, and it's opened me to recognize similar blessings in other difficult situations. Thank you.

RELATIONSHIPS DON'T
GET EASIER;
WE JUST GET MORE
PREPARED BECAUSE
WE BECOME MORE AWARE.

30 NOT EVERYONE WE LOSE IS A LOSS

Like most of us, I usually want everyone to like me, and I move accordingly. This was especially true when I was younger. I believed that if I conducted myself in a certain way, I would be hater-proof. This desire wasn't simply birthed out of some innate need to people-please; it was grounded in how I learned to navigate the neighborhood I grew up in. Don't give people reasons to come at you, and you'll have less trouble to deal with. Anyone in my school who tried to be extra flashy ended up being a target to rob. By high school, I saw the loudest mouths eat the most fists, so we picked our battles and were good to people, in hopes they would be good to us. So I didn't rock the boat and tried desperately to be liked. I wanted to be able to say, "I don't have any haters."

When I first started releasing music to the public, I went through their comments with a fine-tooth comb to see all the ways people took in my work. If they found something offensive, I was quick to defend myself, hoping to win them back. When it comes to being a creative, Toronto is one of the more difficult cities to win over; that's why there's a regular pattern of Toronto-born artists finding their shine outside of the city before being seen as a hometown hero. So I was particularly cautious about rocking the boat and being seen as inauthentic, because I didn't want to become a target for hate.

One day I got a text from a friend letting me know that another rapper from the next neighborhood over (and with whom I had never had any problems) had taken shots at me in a new song.

"Naw, he's not talking about me man, we've been good since the jump. You're reading too much into this."

"No man, he mentioned you by name!"

My mind started racing in confused circles.

When was the last time I had even seen him? It'd been well over a year.

I just texted one his best friends a month ago, and that was a boring conversation about studio equipment.

Why is he dissing me?

I listened to the song and watched the video, and my heart sank. Not because he got me good, or because this was going to affect my career, but because I still had no idea why this was happening. Why didn't he like me anymore? What did I do? How many other people feel this way about me?

I started remembering all the other friends who had betrayed me in the past and the horrible feelings that came with that.

Am I a bad person?

Do I deserve this?

Have I gone soft?

Is success making me a target?

The questions were endless, and the people reaching out to me to help figure out what was going on felt the same. Young dudes from my neighborhood were offering to find him for me, mutual friends were trying to get the lowdown to feed their inner gossip queens, and the online audience was looking forward to seeing some blood.

But I was in no mood; this wasn't fun for me, and it hurt. I had no idea what I had done to provoke the attack, and that consumed me more than figuring out how to address him. His best friend gave me no sign there was a problem. It was killing me to figure out why he took shots at me.

It doesn't matter why someone did something to us as much as it matters why we care.

None of us enjoys finding out when others don't like us, especially when we can't think of anything we did to make them feel that way. We all enjoy acceptance and validation. And yet, we can't control the reactions of others. This guy's attacks on me were more of a reflection of him than they were of me. The truth is, we're allowed to have people not like us, and sometimes we have to say good-bye to those people.*

I cared that this person didn't like me, but I didn't have a good reason to. He had a history of attracting the wrong type of energy and attention, and this was one of many examples of his putting more toxicity into the world.

I was better off without him.

Not every person we lose in life is a loss. Of course, it hurt to know that the last time I saw him or his friends, they were only pretending to be friendly and were really talking shit behind my back. Knowing this brought up other difficulties I'd had with friends in the past and initially made me want to throw up my guard and subscribe to a new set of trust issues. But if I did that, then I would have lost the real battle: me vs. myself.

We can't make everyone happy, ever, and trying to is such a waste of time, energy, love, and focus. If we don't have great chemistry with someone, that's okay—we can't win 'em all, and we shouldn't.

---

* Or accept their good-bye, in my case.

You can be the ripest, juiciest peach in the world, and there's still going to be somebody who hates peaches.

—Dita Von Teese

I lost someone I considered a friend that day, and I never bothered to reply with my own diss track or attempt to reconcile. He could have the victory and the fan base that salivates for drama—none of that is important to me, I'm better off without all of them.

I stopped worrying about people liking me. I also didn't descend into a world of trust issues. Instead, I doubled down on my trust for myself. I trust that no matter what happens, I will be able to handle and address it. If someone doesn't want to be in my life, and they communicate that to me in a passive-aggressive way, that's fine; I'm better off not having their energy in my life and lucky that at least I know where they stand. It would be worse to have them remain around me with fake hugs and smiles.

Losing people is hard, but losing ourselves while trying to keep others happy is much more expensive. We can't please everyone, but we can stay true to ourselves. There's no point in having everyone like us if we don't like ourselves.

Not everything we lose is a loss; often, losing something makes room for us to recognize who and what we really value in life.

LOSING PEOPLE IS HARD,
BUT LOSING OURSELVES
WHILE TRYING TO
KEEP OTHERS HAPPY IS
MUCH MORE EXPENSIVE.

31 WE CAN LOSE MORE TRYING TO WIN

I had surprised my parents with a trip to the Masai Mara in Kenya to take a safari and do some volunteer work, and now we were at the airport to head home. The trip had been flawless, and I was looking forward to hibernating for the first leg of the flight home. I had bought upgraded seats for our trip, the first time I had ever done so out of my own pocket, but it felt worth it for sixteen hours of travel after an amazing ten-day adventure. Yet luxury had to wait: Our flight was delayed, and my parents and I soon found ourselves in a room full of frustrated travelers.

When they finally called the groups up to board, they called Platinum and Gold members first. We were Gold, so we walked up and were the first in line. I was wearing a sweatshirt, sweatpants, and a beanie on my head.* A man in an expensive suit walked up to the line and politely said "Excuse me" as he tried to walk by.

In my most polite Canadian accent, I interjected, "Sorry man, we're in line to board."

Taken aback, he dismissively replied, "Yes, they called me first, I'm Platinum."

---

* This was my sleep-on-the-plane outfit.

With a slight pause to compose myself, I responded, "Yeah, they called Platinum *and* Gold, and we're Gold. This is the line for Platinum and Gold."

Annoyed, he said, "Let me see your ticket," pointing to the section that said Platinum on his. "See, I paid more than you, and that's why I'm boarding first."

Listen, you bougie pretentious ass mutherfucker, watch how you fucking speak to me in front of my family. I don't give a fuck how much you paid for your fuckin' ticket, and what you think you're entitled to. Get the fuck outta my face before I headbutt you.

I calmly replied, "Listen man, I understand, but she said Gold and Platinum, and we're Gold, and that's why we're here. I'm not sure why you're turning this into an argument."

This further annoyed the businessman. He popped out his chest and was about to reply when another passenger interjected. He got between us, and with the most responsible adult posture he said to me, "Sir, I'm sorry this man is being an embarrassment. I have no idea why he's acting like this. You can have my place in line."

The businessman had his moment of clarity, his body language slumped down, and he apologized.

"I'm sorry, I was frustrated, I embarrassed myself."

You better fuckin' apologize, acting like you're better than people because you got more money. Can't you see I'm with two older people? What the fuck is your problem?

This guy had already hit a nerve for me. I've had previous experiences like this flying first class when I wasn't dressed "the part." To be honest, I never understood how people flew in suits; I always thought pajamas would make the trip more comfortable, regardless of the seat.

But I did my best to calm down, saying, "It's okay man. We're all hot and tired. I just wanted you to know we weren't trying to go before our turn."

Boarding began, and we all took our seats. I was embarrassed that my parents had to see the conflict. My mother was very annoyed by the exchange, and at our transfer eight hours later in Germany, she was still talking about it. The truth was, I was also still annoyed. I couldn't let go of how disrespectful the man had been to me and my family, but I was also beginning to feel bad for holding onto it for that long.

The grudge I was holding on to reminded me of an old Zen story I read. Once upon a time an old monk and his young disciple were walking past a wealthy woman standing next to a large puddle of water and mud. Nobody was available to carry her across the water, so the old monk lifted her up and carried her to the other side. It was quick and quiet. The woman got off, didn't thank the monk, and continued on her way. The young disciple was shocked.

Several miles down the road, the young disciple was still upset over the incident. "That woman was so rude," he began. "You were kind enough to carry her across the puddle and she didn't even thank you!"

The old monk replied, "I put that woman down a long time ago. Why are you still carrying her?"

I'm not big on zodiacs, but as a Cancer, I definitely hold grudges. Many people have wronged me in the past, and I've spent more time than I want to admit reliving those experiences, plotting my revenge, and wishing for bad things to happen to them. But I failed to realize that the only person truly affected by all that toxicity was me.

My grudges don't always manifest themselves in labeling others as the enemy. Sometimes it's a dull resentment that plays out as passive-aggressive behavior* or simply being a hater.**

Coexisting with other people means we're going to have friction and conflict. I grew up in a Punjabi Sikh household; both heritages have a rich history of warfare and conflict, and I was raised with a fair amount of exposure to that. Steve Jobs noted that friction is what polishes and smooths rocks, and it's the same with people, so we shouldn't avoid it. But he never said anything about holding a grudge. Some difficult situations are unavoidable, but we all have the choice to let that shit go. We can embrace the friction that occurs between people without holding the grudge.

I doubt I'll ever come across that businessman again, nor do I think he was a bad person. He was just someone who was tired and frustrated with the delays like most of us in that cramped gate, and he wanted to be sure that the extra money he had paid got him the perks he expected. Who among us wouldn't have that same expectation? We all have a tipping point, and I'm sure our conflict was his proverbial straw that broke that camel's back.

I, on the other hand, was in a good mood before the conflict, and thus I didn't have to express any of the italic sentiments I shared earlier. That inner monologue came from a place that, at the end of the day, was all about wanting to win the argument with that man. But I was the only one who would have ended up suffering for it. We can be right in an argument and still lose, because we wasted time arguing. The italic side of me was my ego wanting to be validated. My biggest enemy in that situation wasn't the man in the suit; it was my insecurities and my need to prove myself. Trying to win that battle

---

* Also toxic.
** Toxic too.

with him would have put me further behind in the challenges I face in trying to make myself a better person.

Digging ourselves in and trying to win when the fight isn't worth it can end up costing us much more than a bruise to the ego. **The tunnel vision that comes from trying to satisfy our egos can lead us into great danger.** I've seen people with chips on their shoulders almost throw away all of their blessings to prove one person wrong; it's not worth it. We have to be mindful of the battles we pick, with people around us and within ourselves.

As I already mentioned, Sikh culture places a lot of emphasis on the warrior, but that's not simply fighting oppression in the world—it's about recognizing and fighting our own enemies within, ego being the biggest of them.

Some people neglect their families or personal health to get juicier paychecks. Others damage their relationships with their friends to be accepted by the "cool kids" in circles they have no business being around. **Everything we want comes at a cost, whether that cost is our time, energy, attention, or love, so we need to ask ourselves whether any of that is worth trading away for the thing we're chasing.**

It wasn't worth it to me to win an argument at an airport. I would have lost more than I won, and that's taken me a few instances to realize.[*]

This experience reminded me of my tendency to hold grudges— another energy sucker. Maybe it's the Cancer in me, or just a deep-seated frustration with myself that I couldn't do more in that situation. Looking back at it now, I may have lost the battle, but I won a lifetime of learning and maintained my composure around my parents. I'll

---

[*] Blanket apologies to my exes.

have plenty of opportunities to make up for it with the new tools that experience gifted me.

I've cut myself slack, not just with that conflict, but in other areas where I've mistaken my stubbornness for resilience. I no longer want to lose to gain, unless I have a clear and closer look at what the cost of that's going to be. Social media, and society as a whole, celebrate winners but rarely allow you to see all the sacrifices the winners make. I bet if you saw all those sacrifices, you wouldn't want to be a winner at half the shit other people are celebrating.

SOME DIFFICULT SITUATIONS
ARE UNAVOIDABLE, BUT
WE ALL HAVE THE CHOICE
TO LET THAT SHIT GO.

32 FREEDOM IS HAVING NOTHING TO LOSE

I took some nighttime cold medicine and boarded a fourteen-hour flight to Hong Kong. I fell asleep before the plane had finished boarding. A considerate flight attendant woke me up eight hours later so I didn't miss another meal. As I slowly regained my senses, the woman sitting beside me gave me a smile and said, "I've been waiting for you to wake up so we can talk."

Okay, so I'm still asleep and this is a dream, because who says that?! Okay, this is not a dream, it's real. Was she staring at me the whole time I slept? What does she want to talk to me about? Do I have drool in my beard?

Surprised, I replied, "Oh, so what did you want to talk about?" as the food came our way. She was an older German woman and had a posture and poise that reminded me of Jane Fonda. She told me she was a retired flight attendant and now she travels to East Asia to train other flight attendants. Her energy was very warm, and she spoke only of things that made her eyes widen.

I told her I was headed to Bali to spend time and try to reconnect/relapse with someone who had dumped me a year before.* The

---

* You read about her in chapter 5.

woman celebrated my decision and regaled me with some of her adventures of love, heartbreak, and reconnection.

Then she spoke of her parents and her mother's attempts to reconnect with her father years after they had been separated in concentration camps in World War II Germany.

"You're a Holocaust survivor!?" I was wide awake now, not realizing how loud I just asked that question. Here I was sitting beside someone who had overcome one of the most horrific moments in human history, and I spent half our time together asleep.

She shared that she was around six years old when she and her mother were separated from her father and sent to internment camps in and around Germany. She had only a handful of memories, but she said it took almost four years for them to be reunited. It's rare to meet a survivor of the Holocaust, and even rarer to find out that both her parents survived as well. Many of her uncles and aunts did not.

She asked me about myself. I had just left teaching a few weeks before and told her about my goals as an artist, the music I made, the things I wrote, and the topics I discussed. She seemed genuinely interested and even wrote down my information so she could look me up later.

We talked about freedom, an idea that had drastically different meanings for the two of us. Here I was trying to live a life centered around my passions, spoiled to be on the privileged side of the pond where I could explore my artistic side; and there she was, a survivor who, as a child, had seen the ugliest things humans can do.

I spoke about the activism that was close to my heart, and the people I wish could be free, and she replied with something so profound that I had it carved into my skin several years later:

Freedom is having nothing to lose.

People find freedom when they have nothing left to lose; once they decide to risk everything for their freedom, they've achieved that freedom. The oppressed are freed when they stop asking for freedom and take it. If they die doing so, they at least die free.

> It is better to die on your feet than to live on your knees!
>
> —Dolores Ibarruri (La Pasionaria)

Every one of us has a list of things to lose, a list of failures to avoid, a list of fears we don't want to cross paths with. It's a list of cages we hold the keys to but still feel claustrophobic within. We aspire for more, to be free from this all, without ever realizing that the freedom we want starts with us and requires no one else's permission or validation. The moment we decide to fight for our freedom, even if it costs us our lives, we've already become free.

Once we decide, we become. It's easier said than done, but not if you mean it.

Getting to a point of having nothing to lose may have happened because we ran out of things to lose, or because we decided that we're no longer going to let the idea of loss scare us into paralysis. Either way, we're free.

When this woman shared her message with me on that flight, it had been only a few weeks since I had started my journey into full-time artistry, blissfully ignorant of the pitfalls and obstacles that were awaiting me. Her words helped me the most when I found myself in the dumps a year later—broke, betrayed, heartbroken, contemplating jumping off my balcony, too embarrassed, ashamed, and scared to face the world.

When we hit our lowest moments, sometimes it's because we

have nothing left to lose. Sometimes we think we've hit rock bottom before we have, and that second fall makes it even harder; but once we've truly hit our lowest point, we're free.

We're free to do anything and everything we want. I decided I was free to be Humble the Poet—even if only for a few months—once I was in the dirt. But I was able to make that decision only because I didn't have anything to lose. Living free as Humble the Poet for a short time was worth more than fifty more years of being anything less.

All the things I usually feared were my oppressors trying to keep me in line, but after this chance meeting, I tried to no longer let those oppressors rule me. I wanted to be free. I told myself it was possible and changed my thinking patterns.

I am free of the embarrassment of being in debt because I trusted the wrong people.

I am free of the betrayal and trust issues I experienced after people hurt me because I can let go of all the resentment. It no longer has permission to weigh me down.

I am free of the misery that comes with heartbreak. I will spill that pain on the page every time it happens—to learn from it, grow from it, and connect with others through it.

I have nothing to lose. If everything must go, then go. I am free now and forever.

The moment we decide to learn from our losses, we no longer feel them or fear them. And once we are free from the fear of loss, we are free to discover ourselves and live our most authentic lives.

I am eternally grateful to the flight attendant who woke me up so I could meet the retired German flight attendant sitting next to me. I'm not sure what I did to deserve the beautiful experiences I continue to have, so the best thing I can think of is to share them all with you, my handsome friends.

Each of you reading this book is fighting your own battles; some of you feel cornered against the ropes, on the defense, or you're just trying to weather the storm. I've been there, wishing for the simpler times, overwhelmed with all that is happening, feeling emotions that seem two sizes too big for my body. I can't take those struggles away from you or jump in the ring for you; to be honest, I wouldn't even if I could.

Instead, I would stand in your corner, and at the top of my lungs I would remind you of everything you've endured up to this point, and that you're still here. That's more than enough proof that not only can you survive what you're going through now, you can get out of that corner, start throwing some punches, and thrive. Let everyone, including yourself, know that you're not afraid to get knocked down, or even knocked out, as long as you go down fighting.

Once that flight landed, I never heard from that woman again, and I never got a chance to thank her for uttering simple words that forever transformed my perspective. She survived and thrived well beyond anything my journey has thrown my way, and I'm forever grateful that our paths crossed.

THE MOMENT WE DECIDE
TO LEARN FROM OUR LOSSES,
WE NO LONGER FEEL THEM
OR FEAR THEM.

33

THERE ARE NO TIME MACHINES, SO FIX IT NEXT TIME

Every Christmas season, Lilly does "12 Collabs of Christmas," a video series with celebrities and public figures to celebrate the end of the year. Reaching out to the celebs to get them to be a part of the project takes months of notice, and of course, quickly scheduled changes, so Lilly and her team are left to make last-minute scrambles to make the videos happen.

One celebrity who doesn't pose too many challenges for Lilly is the magnificent Dwayne "The Rock" Johnson, former wrestler turned Hollywood superstar. The Rock has been a central figure in Lilly's life, and that has spilled its way into mine. I met him a few times at events, Lilly and I have had the chance to watch him work his magic on set, and I even participated in his version of the viral Mannequin Challenge in 2016.

Lilly invited The Rock to participate in one of her twelve collabs, and he agreed, but it would have to be in Hawaii since he was working on a project there. Lilly invited me to join her and the team in Hawaii, but I couldn't take her up on the offer. As much as I wanted to, I wasn't in a position to afford tickets to fly across the ocean just to watch Lilly shoot a video with The Rock. Every experience I had with him left me inspired, but my fears attached to my thin wallet at the time held me back. I wished her luck on the video and stayed home in Toronto.

Things didn't go as planned in Hawaii, and some of the additional talent Lilly had expected to co-star with The Rock couldn't make it, so she had no choice but to have her day-to-day manager, Kyle, sit in to fill the role. So Kyle, who prefers to be behind the camera, got the chance to play The Rock's best friend in front of it instead.

Had I been there, that would have been me. I would have had the opportunity to act alongside one of the nicest people to ever dominate Hollywood, and I couldn't because I was home, freezing my butt off in Toronto instead.

The FOMO was real.

As I sat there watching the finished product and picturing myself in the role and kicking myself, I made a decision that not only melted the FOMO, but also allowed me some clarity moving forward when similar situations arose.

I promised myself never to deny myself a new experience, regardless of the cost.

Now lucky for me, I don't have expensive tastes or habits, and most of these opportunities that come my way involve travel and being around unique people in unique situations. So I reasoned that the debt from travel would eventually be paid off, and the memory and impact of the experiences would last forever.

This promise to myself came with another unexpected perk: It made me realize I'd held myself back from new things sometimes because of fear, not just the cost. So I did what I could to break the pattern. Sometimes moving past the fear meant spending money; other times it meant getting out of the house; and other times it meant being brave enough to be open and honest in my communication.

I no longer regret missing that opportunity to act alongside The Rock. Missing out was the kick in the butt I needed to ensure something like that would never happen again. I've said "yes" to invites and trips since, all out of pocket, and have yet to regret any of those decisions.

The lesson I learned from missing out is one that has stayed with me. There was no point in being bitter about it; I simply decided to get better by making better decisions that suit my priorities.

We all make mistakes, and when things don't go in our favor, we can end up stewing in regret. But nothing comes from that. **There are no time machines, so fix it next time.** This principle applies not only to our choices, but also to the work we put out. So many of us are paralyzed in a world of perfectionism because we're afraid of making a mistake. The first two editions of my book *Unlearn* had spelling and grammatical errors, but the world didn't end. I found the mistakes and fixed them for the next editions. When I find mistakes in my music videos, I don't take them down or obsess. I take notes and make sure not to make the same errors the next time. That's all we can do: move on with the new knowledge and wisdom we acquire from the mistakes of our past.

I don't regret not going to Hawaii as much as I regret letting fear make its way into my decisions. I remember how I felt after the fact—frustrated and envious—and now any time fear creeps its way back into my decision-making process, I do my best to recognize it so I don't make the same mistake twice. If missing that once-in-a-lifetime opportunity left me with nothing but this resolve to not let fear get in the way again, it's a fair trade.

Regrets take their toll on us, and they do very little to help us move forward. It's up to us to shift our perspectives to find a lesson so we're not doomed to repeat the same mistake again.

THAT'S ALL WE CAN DO:
MOVE ON WITH THE NEW
KNOWLEDGE AND WISDOM
WE ACQUIRE FROM
THE MISTAKES OF OUR PAST.

CLOSE

The idea of being opportunistic sounds sleazy—we think of a shady car salesman with greasy hair and an uncomfortable smile. But we have to reclaim the idea. I encourage you to pay attention to how life will provide you with ample opportunity to reevaluate everything, from your principles and morals to your expectations, as you have new experiences. Opportunism for me now means recognizing my power to find opportunity in any situation instead of simply labeling the situation as a win or a loss. That's why it's important to exercise our muscles of perception to see situations from as many angles as possible.

By the time this book comes out, it will have gone through hundreds of hours of revisions and rewrites, and all I'll want for that work is for the book to "do well." That can mean anything from making the *New York Times* bestseller list to simply inspiring some readers who might use their newfound powers to help direct the world into a better place. Regardless of how this book does commercially, or critically,* I know that I've already become a better writer through the process. I've learned to focus my ideas and explore myself on a deeper level, and no money or accolades in the world can compare with the fact that I'm getting better at my craft.

---

* If that even matters.

In any case, I'll be prepared with pen and pad in hand to take notes and see what worked with this book, what didn't work, and what the best next steps will be. If need be, I'll allow myself some time to feel bad before moving forward, but what I won't be is merely reactive. Learning to see the opportunities in everything has prepared me to be more proactive.

There are so many times in all of our lives when things go exactly according to plan, only to leave us disappointed a short time later. There are also moments when the exact opposite of our expectations occurs, and later on, it turns out to be the best thing ever. **Focusing on the lessons in our failures and shortcomings ensures that things will always have a silver lining, and that's the recipe for sustainable success moving forward.**

I feel very fortunate to be able to learn not only from my mistakes, but also from the mistakes of others. To learn from mistakes, we have to spend more time actively paying attention and adjusting our perspectives accordingly. When we've spent time on this planet paying attention, we notice a lot of patterns in the way that existence governs itself.

Exercise sucks in the short term but has great long-term benefits. Eating one hundred French fries in minutes is wonderful in the short term but does a lot of long-term damage. The same applies to life. Sometimes, losing people may sting in the short term, but we're better off in the long term. The same applies to the times our expectations aren't met. When we truly absorb this idea, failures are no longer the enemy, something to be avoided. Even when things don't go our way and we suffer, we can hold onto that experience as a valuable lesson not to repeat history and can chalk up the unpleasantness to the cost of learning the game.

We can't trust a world we can't control, but we can trust our-

selves to handle things with our elevated perspectives and magical powers to see the opportunity in everything. I've met people who got rich even after the stock market crashed, and artists who found creative workarounds to the limitations of their art. The world always needs new ideas, and new ideas come from people who are looking for them, not from people who are busy judging what's in front of them. If we adapt and adjust to the world, we'll find ourselves more in synch and flow with the things that happen around us.

The podcaster and entrepreneur Tim Ferriss made a very simple template to help us find opportunity in any outcome. He suggests that every time we think of a "what-if" that holds us back from moving forward, we simply decide how we can prevent that fear from occurring and how to repair it if it does. This can apply to the fear of not getting a good seat at a movie theater for an opening-night show, all the way to quitting a salaried job in order to start a pet-grooming business. Sometimes, playing out the scenarios in our heads in order to preempt potential pitfalls not only sets us up for success, it also ensures that we're not as paralyzed with fear and that we're more prepared for complications after we take that first step.

There's a quote associated with the American artist Florence Scovel Shinn: "No man is your friend, no man is your enemy, every man is your teacher."

I think we can update this to be less gendered and more applicable for life generally: "No situation is good, no situation is bad, every situation is our teacher."

The moment we can learn from a situation is the moment we win, finding and creating shiny gold in even the dullest and dimmest of places.

Exit

It's not a loss, it's a lesson
All the things we've been stressing
Have been tearing us down, and building us right back up

Like muscle fibers, our heart is resilient
Learning from our loss, creates a life of brilliance

Learning from our losses, is earning from our losses
And those rewards are priceless

Thank you for taking from me to give me more

OUTRO

This is not the part of the book where I wrap everything up in a neat and tidy bow. This is the part of the book where I remind you that life is more complicated than that. The best we can do is make lemonade, yet sometimes life throws us things that we can't make sense of right away. Some experiences—particularly our traumas—are works in progress.

A while back, someone I loved revealed to me that she had been raped. We were in the middle of The Fight to End All Fights, and at the height of it she told me what had happened to her.

There was no Humble the Poet twist in perspective to that experience. It was a moment when shit got realer than real, and everything we thought was a problem instantly lost its priority.

In moments like that—when life isn't just unfair, but it's cruel—we can't help but notice there's no fairytale ending. One of the things no one else could teach me is the fact that life doesn't always work like that. Yet the silver lining is that even when there isn't a perfect resolution, there can be healing and self-exploration. We can choose to see our broken heart as an open heart that is willing to grow and mend. Once we focus on seeking what no one else can teach us, we become students of life.

Despite all that I've encountered, all that I've learned, and all that I've shared, I, like you, will forever be figuring things out. The famous proverb tells us: "Give a man a fish, and he will eat for a day. Teach a man to fish, and he will eat for a lifetime." I didn't write this book to hand you a fish, but rather to show you the tools you've always had that empower you to fish for yourself. There's still going to be a boatful of things that no one else can teach you and me, and we're going to have to continue figuring it all out ourselves. But that doesn't mean we have to do it alone.

I still wrestle with knowing that someone I love went through such an awful trauma as rape. This won't heal quickly for me or for her. But I do know that for her, speaking her truth to me was a part of her healing process. It was the first time she had ever said it out loud, she later admitted, and it helped her make sense of something that had made no sense when it happened. She, like many victims of sexual assault, carried the burden alone for years, scared of any shaming or judgment that could potentially come from sharing her story.

With her blessing, I share her story with you. This messy, painful story feels more like a journey than a destination, yet I share it because, even though there is so much we have to figure out on our own, we have to share our stories. **There is so much power in realizing we're not alone.**

What I told you at the beginning of this book is still true: I couldn't show you how to feel better about your unique experiences even if I wanted to.* I can only share mine and show you how I'm figuring out my shit.

I don't have a perfect life, and I don't have all the answers, and I still encounter bullshit in epic proportions. Like you, I'm going to have to slowly figure it out the hard way, the slow way, the patient way, and the very uncomfortable way. But that journey involves friends

---

* I would if I could.

and helpers who are there for me, and my being there for them. We don't have to do this alone. Let's trade stories, notes, best practices, triumphs, failures, and everything in between.

You're not going to close this book with a feeling of completion and satisfaction; you're going to close this book with resolve to answer my call to action.

The reason there are things no one else can teach us is because no one else can live our lives and explore our stories for us. **All of our lives are beautiful messes, and no one else knows how it feels to have our experiences, or how much we hold onto, or how much longer we can go on.**

You've seen me work through my stories to change the way I see things and ultimately move forward better equipped for the next challenge. I implore you to do the same: Make sense of your own self, and help others who may be in your shoes.

Day by day it feels like nothing changes, but when we look back, we realize how much has changed and how much progress we've made.

Unfortunately, in many communities, lots of these topics are taboo. This makes us afraid to share, even though sharing could save countless other people who are going through the same things. So let's flood the world with our stories to help equip, empower, and embolden others to feel a little less alone. This is how we've been doing it since the beginning of our history. Not all the stories will be pleasant or easy to tell, but they're all important to share, because they're all important to hear.

It's okay to feel, it's okay to cry.

This book isn't simply something I wanted to do, it's something I had to do. I had to do this for those looking for something to connect to, to relate to, so that they can feel less alone. More important, I had to do this for myself, to face myself and make sense of myself. I had to do this to understand how my story so far has shaped me, and how I can shape the rest of it.

I want you to do the same with yours.

If you made it this far, then you can help take this even farther. Please tell your stories in any way or fashion you choose, whether you sing them out, paint them on, write them down, dance them off, or sculpt them away. It doesn't matter how you share, because your stories—all our stories—are essential and will find a way to connect.

There are jewels to be found, discovered, or created in every story. This is something no one else can teach us, but we can figure it out together.

ACKNOWLEDGMENTS

This goes out to you, and you, and you, and you.

Thank you for making time with me, and not skipping the acknowledgments, a part of the book where we often see a list of names we don't recognize, or a list of celebrities I'm pretending to be friends with.

I would not be where I am on this journey if it wasn't for you, so I would love to thank you, acknowledge you, and give you a bushy-bearded kiss.

I appreciate you for riding with me in all the ways you do.